UNVEILING *THE* APOCALYPSE

BY
DR. GLENYCE DOORN

The following is an in-depth devotional study of the Book of Revelation, The Apocalypse, taken from the notes, syllabus, and recordings of teachings given by Dr. Glenyce Doorn, PhD at the International School of Ministry of the Endtime Handmaidens at Engeltal, Arkansas, United States of America.

For more books:
Send an email request to radoorn@juno.com

All Scripture references are from the HOLY BIBLE, KING JAMES VERSION, ©1972, 1976, 1979, 1983, 1984, 1985, Thomas Nelson Inc.

Disclaimer: Certain Scripture references from the KJV my contain underlining, capitalization, or inserts in parenthesis with emphasis added by the author.

Unveiling the Apocalypse by Dr. Glenyce Doorn

CONTENTS

CHAPTERS

MEMORIAL

This woman of God, Glenyce Irene Salseth, was born into a humble farm family on a snowy Wisconsin day on February 22,1930 at 2pm near the Norwegian village of Woodville, Saint Croix county, Wisconsin. Her father, Eckhard Oliver Salseth, and her mother, Gladys Selina Nichols Salseth, both had become Christians through the efforts of the local Norwegian Baptist Church. She was raised in a loving Christian home.

After many years of faithful members of their little Baptist Church, they heard of a group of Pentecostal Christian's who were starting a church in their area. They joined this group of Pentecostals at that time and this became their faith for the rest of their lives.

Glenyce enrolled in North-Central Bible Institute in Minneapolis, Minnesota. It was there she first saw a young student from Michigan by the name of Bob Doorn. During the summer of 1949 in Bob's home church in Grand Rapids, Bob and Glenyce were the best man and maid of honor in their best friends' wedding. Going down the aisle together following the ceremony, they met for the first time. Following brief introductions, and after only walking a few steps, the Spirit of God spoke to Bob's heart and said "this girl will one day become your wife." In God's appointed time it all came together, and on July 25, 1950 they were wed at Church that they first pastored together, the Wilson Community Church in Wilson, Wisconsin.

After 40 years of successful pastoring, the Doorns embarked on full-time missionary ministry to the nations of the world doing ministry on every continent except Australia. During these years God blessed them with three wonderful children, Timothy, Mark, and Susan along with eight precious grandchildren. Mama Doorn is resting in the arms of Jesus until that day when we are all reunited by the grace of God in the precious blood of Jesus. Her prayer was that this book would be a blessing to all who read it.

FOREWORD

In 2005, I traveled to Michigan to minister at Open Door Worship Center, pastored by Dale Scholten. It was an incredible meeting and it's became an annual meeting for a number of years. It was there I met Papa and Mama Doorn, seasoned ministers and missionaries, who just happens to live in Florida about one hour and thirty minutes from me.

I met them often for lunch to share stories of God's work in the ministry. During our time together, we realized that God had a word for the church concerning the Revelation of John. Mama had taught this material for years, and in 2010 her dream to publish her teaching into a book, Unveiling the Apocalypse, became a reality.

On October 28, 2019, at the age of 89, mom and Doorn went to be with the Lord. I attended the funeral in Orlando, FL, and reached out to papa through his son, Mark. All of mamas books were sold and the book was out of print.

So, I am very excited to see her book in reprint. You will be blessed as you read her life's work.

Dr. Paul A. Moore

PREFACE

It is with great joy that I am privileged to Preface this unusual book written by my beloved bride of six decades. I sat by her side to occasionally add my so-called "two cents " as she had labored so diligently on searching out the truth of the interpretation of the Apocalypse, the Book of Revelation.

Beside her lounge chair, where she so frequently studied, was a stack of books, commentaries and the like, regarding this sacred book. Many of them are old and very scholarly, but unbelievably they were all saying the same thing. It seemed that down through the years one just copied what the other one said with rarely a new idea on the various interpretations of what God was trying to tell us in the last book of His Holy Word.

Finally she said to me one day, after weeks of continual study, "I'm just going to have to get this thing to prayer and search the original text because I know there is more than what all these books are trying to tell me." So she began her deep quest for what the Word of God was really saying.

It is a sure thing that I learned things that I never knew before even after teaching and preaching the Word of God for some 60 years. Our favorite professor in Bible college, Dr. T.J. Jones, taught us this: "Never tackle the book of Revelation until you have been in ministry at least twenty years, then never try to explain Chapter 12." We had always been accustomed to the general dispensation teaching on Revelation so we just assumed that all we had been taught in Bible college and seminary was absolute truth. Come to find out, they also had been following all the old commentaries without finding for themselves whether something was really the correct interpretation or not.

I am excited to present to you on behalf of my Beloved the prospect of causing God's people to search deeper for the truth regarding the End Times and the coming of our Lord Jesus Christ for his overcoming church. My prayer is that you will be stimulated and stirred by the study of this book and it will cause you to want more than ever to be an "Overcomer," which is the truth theme of the book of Revelation. Therefore I am pleased to present to you my wife's masterpiece, Unveiling the Apocalypse.

Dr. Robert "Papa" Doorn, Ph.D.

INTRODUCTION

The author of the Book of Revelation is the Apostle John according to Revelation 1:1. He is the same John who authored the Gospel of John and the three Epistles of John. It is interesting to note that John lived a full life in the service of Christ and died a natural death at 94 years of age in the City of Ephesus. All of the other eleven apostles were killed or martyred included Judas Iscariot who hanged himself after betraying our Lord.

Revelation means, "to take the cover off". Revelation is the uncovering of the Glory of Jesus Christ and of that which the future holds. The first verse of the book speaks about *"things which must shortly come to pass"*. The past 2,000 years is not a short amount of time. Strong's Greek Concordance (#5038) essentially does not mean *"at once"* or *"in a very short time to come"*. It rather means that, when it happens, it will come about *"with speed, swiftly or quickly"*. When Christ's coming takes place at the end of time, it will happen *"In a moment, in the twinkling of an eye, at the last trump; for the trumpet shall sound, and the dead shall be raised incorruptible, and we shall be changed!"* (I Cor. 15:52).

John, the apostolic writer, was taken captive and placed on the Isle of Patmos, a totally forsaken place, to die because of his testimony of the Lord Jesus Christ according to Revelation 1:9. John was chosen by God to see heaven and tell the story of those things which will come to pass. This is why he declares, *"I was in the Spirit on the Lord's Day, and heard behind me a great voice as of a trumpet."* (Rev. 1:10). This was not Sunday which is often referred to as "The Lord's Day" or even Saturday, the Jewish Sabbath. It was the day of the visitation of the Lord Jesus Christ who gave John, through the mighty angel, the sights and words we call Revelation, the Apocalypse.

The Spirit of the Lord told John to write about the things that he had seen which are now and the things, which were to come hereafter. John saw seven candlesticks, better translated as "lampstands" that could burn continually. Standing in their midst was One like unto the Son of Man. John remembered Him well as he was there with Him on the Mount of Transfiguration. John saw Him as the great High Priest who serves at the right hand of the Majesty on High. John describes His garments and His beautiful features. The sight is so awesome that John falls at His feet as one dead. It is then that he records the first words that Jesus speaks to him. *"Fear not! I am the First and the Last!"*

Out of this experience of being banished on Patmos this great apocalypse happened. We know now, after all these thousands of years, God does not measure time as we do. The signs of the times do let us know that we are truly living in the last days of this age. The Lord is allowing catastrophes to awaken the servants of the Lord that something supernatural is about to take place. We have lived so dispensationally minded. Under the law for 4,000 years and now under grace for some 2,000 years makes us wonder what is coming next.

We are now under grace and not law. If the Lord wants to carry out His grace a little longer, it is His own privilege. It is by grace that He allows others to join the Body of Christ in these last days. God has promised something special for these days. *"And it shall come to pass in the last days, saith God, I will pour out of My Spirit upon all flesh, and your sons and your daughters shall prophesy!"* (Acts 2:17; Joel 2:28). God, in His everlasting mercy, is desirous that all His children be on-fire for Him even in the midst of this lukewarm Laodicean age in which we are living. This is the only way that we can get this job of evangelizing the world accomplished and go on to eternity.

Much of Revelation is something of a riddle or in symbolic pictures to be interpreted in a certain way. In the time it was written it would have been dangerous to speak of rulers or nations by name, hence, other terms and cryptic symbols are thus used. This, of course, is where much of the confusion of interpretation comes in. For example, the Roman Empire ruled the world in John's day. He could not very well have blasted them directly so he chose to use the name of Babylon to thus refer to Rome.

Revelation is the only book of its kind in the New Testament. The Gospels and Acts are narratives or stories. Romans to Jude are epistles or letters. The Book of Revelation is 'The Apocalypse'. The Greek word for apocalypse means an 'uncovering' or an 'unveiling' referring to the unseen realms of heaven and the underworld.

Always remember that it is the revelation, singular, of Jesus Christ. It is never used in the plural form, revelations. This glorious book tells us who Jesus is, what Jesus will do, and what Jesus wills to come in the future. The Book of Revelation was not written in chronological order!

REVELATION IS A 'PROPHETIC' WORD

"Blessed is he that readeth, and they that hear the words of this prophesy, and keep those things which are written therein; for the time is at hand." (Rev. 1:3). If ever the time of the apocalypse is at hand, it is now. Look at Revelation 19:10, *"And I fell at His feet to worship Him. And He said unto me, See thou do it not; I am thy fellowservant, and of thy brethren that have the testimony of Jesus; worship God! For the testimony of Jesus is the spirit of prophecy!"* Prophecy is being fulfilled in our day now. When the Lord finally says, "Come home!" this prophecy shall be fully fulfilled.

Revelation 22:7 and 10 declares, *"Behold, I come quickly, blessed is he that keepeth the sayings of the <u>prophecy of this book</u> for the time is at hand...Seal <u>not</u> the saying of the <u>prophecy of this book!</u>"* The reason He says to *"seal it not"* is because it continues until this day and it is not ready to be sealed yet.

Again, John writes, *"For I testify unto every man that heareth the words of the <u>prophecy of this book;</u> if any man shall add unto these things, God shall add unto him the plagues that are written in this book; and if any man shall take away from the words of the <u>book of this prophecy,</u> God shall take away his part out of the book of life, and out of the holy city, and from the things which are written in this book."* (Rev. 22:18-20).

There is something about Revelation that makes us feel as if Christ is coming now and that the time is at hand. The book is written in this light. We must always remember that it is prophetic and the prophecy will be fulfilled without question. We can only look at the times and the signs for we do not know the day nor the hour. We must understand that, even if we have a vision or a dream of the Lord's return, we must not mistake it to mean that He is coming that day or week. The Lord is drawing people to Himself in this last day for He is not willing that any shall be "left behind" or perish.

A BOOK OVER TIME

The Book of Revelation was not accepted for many centuries by the church world even though it was accepted as a canonical book in the New Testament by the Council of Carthage, August 28, 397 A.D. In the great reformation, Martin Luther did not at first accept the Book of Revelation. He placed it with a few other questionable writings in the appendix of his German New Testament published in September of 1522.

John Calvin, the great French Protestant theologian during the reformation, developed the system of Christian theology known as Calvinism or Reformed Theology. He wrote commentaries on nearly all the books of the Bible except the Book of Revelation. Likewise, Zwingli who was the main leader of the Protestant Reformation in Switzerland and founder of the Swiss Reformed Churches declared that Revelation was NOT one of the books of the Bible.

The major opposition to The Book of Revelation by most of these scholars was concerning the doctrine of the Millennium. The debate centered on the idea of it being a literal one thousand year period. Hence, most of these churches are "a-millennial" to this day.

Jerome is best known as the translator of the Bible from Greek and Hebrew into Latin called the Vulgate. He included the Book of Revelation in his translation, which greatly influenced many in the Western world to accept this book. Over time it came to be accepted by the church universal. It is the one book that begins and ends with a blessing to those who read and keep its sayings.

THE FIRST AND THE LAST

The title of this last book in the Bible is 'The Revelation of Jesus Christ'. Revelation is the completion of truth. It dovetails with the book of Genesis as well as with Ezekiel and Daniel.

- Genesis is the book of beginnings. (1:1)

- Revelation the book of consummation. (22:20)

- Genesis speaks of the creation of the heavens and the earth. (2:1)

- Revelation speaks of the New Heaven and the New Earth. (21:1)

- Genesis shows us the first revelation of Satan as the serpent. (3:1)

• Revelation reveals him as *"that old serpent which is the devil and satan"* (Rev. 20:2).

• Genesis shows us the origin of sin. Revelation shows us the finality of sin. *"And the devil that deceived them was cast into the lake of fire."* (Rev. 20:10).

• Genesis speaks of an earthly paradise with the tree of life and the river of God (2:9,10).

• Revelation speaks of *"a pure river of water of life clear as crystal proceeding out of the throne of God and of the Lamb"* and *"the tree of life which bare twelve manner of fruits"* in the heavenly paradise (22:1, 2).

• In Genesis we see man and woman set over the creation of God (2:15).

• In Revelation we see the Last Adam, Jesus, and His Bride ruling over the redeemed world (3:21).

• In Genesis Adam and Eve could not eat of the Tree of Life because of sin (3:22).

• In Revelation the overcoming redeemed will be blessed to eat of the Tree of Life forever (2:7).

• In Genesis we see the first type of the sacrificial lamb (3:21; 22:8).

• In Revelation we see the Lamb once slain sitting in the midst of the throne (5:6).

• In Genesis we see man building his unholy city (11:1).

• In Revelation we see God's Holy City (21:2).

• In Genesis we see sorrow and tears (3:16-19).

• In Revelation we see tears wiped away (21:4).

• In Genesis we see the beginning of night and of darkness (1:14-18).

• In Revelation we see no night there (21:23-25).

In the Book of Ezekiel we again see comparisons:

• Ezekiel, while in captivity, sees a vision of the Lord (1:1).

• In Revelation, while in captivity, John sees a vision of the Lord (1:19).

• In Ezekiel the prophet receives messages for the Jewish people (3:4).

• In Revelation, John receives messages for the seven churches of Asia (1:11).

• Ezekiel sees a vision of the four living creatures around the throne of God (1:5).

• In Revelation, John sees the four living creatures (beasts) around the throne of God (4:6).

• In Ezekiel we see the pronouncement of judgment upon the nations.

• In Revelation we see the nations judged during the tribulation period (Chapters 8, 9).

• Ezekiel sees the coming Messianic Kingdom (Chapters 33 to 37).

• Revelation speaks of the coming Messianic Kingdom. (Chapter 20).

• Ezekiel speaks of the attack of Gog (38, 39).

• Revelation speaks of the attack of Gog and Magog (20:7-10).

• Ezekiel speaks of the vision of the final glory and peace of the redeemed closing with these words, *"The Lord is there!"* (48:35)

• In Revelation we see the final glory and peace of the redeemed closing with these words, *"The grace of our Lord Jesus Christ be with you all!"* (22:21)

THE SEVEN CHURCH AGES

There are various lines of interpretation to the Book of Revelation. Among the major ones are these:

Praeterist – All of the events have already been fulfilled.

Futurist – All of the events are yet to be fulfilled.

Historical – The fulfillment is in the continuous history of the church from John's day until the end of time.

The Book of Revelation is addressed as a general epistle to the Seven Churches of Asia. This Asia in Bible days was a proconsul of the Roman Empire and not our present day Asia as we know it. The present day region is the center of the area where the seven churches were then located. Next to Ephesus, stood the great temple of the goddess Diana where thousands came to worship this false goddess.

While all of the churches of that day were under Roman rule, each church depicted an era of time from then until now. The internal conditions prevailing in those seven churches portray the state of the whole sphere of Christendom in seven time periods from the early church days until the close of the Church Age. The church that Christ declared He would personally build – *"I will build My Church and the gates of hell shall not prevail against it!"* (Matthew 16:18) – has been through all of these time periods beginning with the Apostolic Church of Ephesus through the Philadelphia Church of "Brotherly Love" until our present church age of Laodicea, "The Lukewarm Church".

The Lord Jesus Christ is still building His Church sometimes with a *"very small remnant"* as the Prophet Isaiah tells us in 1:9. He will in the end, however, have an overcoming remnant who shall be, in the words of the Apostle Paul in Ephesians 5:27 – *"A glorious Church not having spot, or wrinkle, or any such thing; but that it should be holy and without blemish!"*

There are two 'church spirits' present in the world today. The first is that of 'Philadelphia', the church of brotherly love and the church that is 'overcoming' by *"the blood of the Lamb and the word of their testimony"*. The other is that of 'Laodicea", the lukewarm spirit of the age which God says He will *"vomit out of His mouth"*. We must *"choose this day whom we will serve"*.

Now, "UNVEILILNG THE APOCALYPSE" - THE REVELATION OF JESUS CHRIST!

CHAPTER 1

THE REVELATION OF JESUS CHRIST

Verses 1-3:

1. *The Revelation of Jesus Christ, which God gave unto him, to shew to his servants things which must shortly come to pass; and he sent and signified it by his angel unto his servant John:*

2. *Who bare record of the Word of God, and of the testimony of Jesus Christ, and of all things that he saw.*

3. *Blessed is he that readeth, and they that hear the words of this prophecy, and keep those things which are written therein: for the time is at hand.*

The Apostle John wrote this Book of Revelation of Jesus Christ, which was given him by God. The Lord Jesus Christ is the one central theme. John is the messenger chosen by God to bring us the truth of God's Divine Revelation.

We are blessed when we read the prophetic words of the end times and seeing things, which will shortly transpire. We are blessed to live in the last Church Age (Laodicea), which brings in the final state of apostasy. Even in this age, God has an overcoming church, which will be ready for His coming. Our real blessing is that we are near to His coming.

And that, knowing the time, that now it is high time to awake out of sleep; for now is our salvation nearer than when we believed.

(Rom. 13:11)

God will open our understanding to this wonderful book if we press through by the Spirit of the Lord.

Verses 4-8:

4. *JOHN to the seven churches which are in Asia: Grace be unto you, and peace, from him which is, and which was, and which is to come, and from the seven Spirits which are before his throne;*

5. *And from Jesus Christ, who is the faithful witness, and the first begotten of the dead, and the Prince of the kings of the earth. Unto him that loved us, and washed us from our sins in his own blood,*

6. *And made us kings and priests unto God and his Father; to him be glory and dominion forever and ever. Amen!*

7. *Behold, he cometh with clouds; and every eye shall see him, and they also which pierced him; and all kindreds of the earth shall wail because of him. Even so, Amen.*

8. *I am Alpha and Omega, the beginning and the ending, saith the Lord, which is, and which was, and which is to come, the Almighty.*

The Lord drew John's attention to Seven Churches of Asia. It is actually Asia Minor or the area of Turkey in our modern time. The Seven Churches there were picked from all the other churches for their unique characteristics. Much of these characteristics would be found in the succeeding ages to come as the destiny of these church ages was fulfilled.

John is the messenger and the actor of the book as he writes what he saw and heard from the angel, from the Lord himself, and from the Seven Spirits, which are before God's throne. These Seven Spirits are perhaps better explained as *"the Seven-fold Spirit"*. These Seven Spirits rest upon the Lord Jesus Christ and are there before the throne to this day. God also promises that they will be *"sent forth into all the earth"* (Rev. 5:6). As we travel the nations in this 21st Century, we are truly seeing the "Seven-fold Spirit" of God at work throughout the nations of the world. God's promises always come to pass.

THE SEVEN SPIRITS OF GOD

And there shall come forth a rod out of the stem of Jesse, and a Branch shall grow out of his roots:

And the Spirit of the Lord shall rest upon him, the spirit of wisdom and understanding, the spirit of counsel and might, the spirit of knowledge and of the fear of the Lord.

(Isa. 11:1,2)

Here the Prophet Isaiah clearly defines the Seven Spirits or Seven-fold Spirit of God, which we find in the Book of Revelation.

1. The Spirit of the Lord.
2. The Spirit of Wisdom.
3. The Spirit of Understanding.
4. The Spirit of Counsel.
5. The Spirit of Might.
6. The Spirit of Knowledge.
7. The Spirit of the Fear (Reverence) of God.

It is the Lord Jesus who is the faithful witness to these Seven Spirits. It is He who has washed us from our sins in His own blood. It is He who has made us kings and priests unto the Lord. Many Christians cannot see themselves as a king or a priest. This does not mean that we will be literal kings and reign over a country or a group of people.

We are to operate spiritually as a king ruling over the forces of evil and resisting the enemy. We are to rule over our flesh and not participate in the things of the world. *To rule means to take our God-given authority and exercise our rights of domain.*

We are to be a priest or one who stands between God and man. As priests, we are to share the gift of salvation even to the nations. Through the royal priesthood, we act as God's mediator offering righteousness to a sinful world, healing to a dying generation and the love of Christ to draw humanity into God's Kingdom. As spiritual priests, we do not rule over the laity which was the *"the doctrine of the Nicolaitanes"* which God said He hated in Revelation 2:15. We are to be soul winners and win the lost for Jesus.

Jesus Christ will one day come and in that Resurrection Day there will be both anguish and rejoicing depending on our condition. Let's not be of those who will *"wail because of Him"*, but of those who will declare *"Even so, come Lord Jesus!"*

ALPHA AND OMEGA

Four times in Revelation, the Lord Jesus is declared to be *"Alpha and Omega"* – in 1:8, 1:11, 21:6 and 22:13. Alpha is the first and Omega the last letter of the Greek alphabet. In the first reference, He is also called *"the beginning and the ending"*. In the second, He is called *"the first and the last"*. In the third instance, He is again declared to be *"the beginning and the end"*. Finally, both terms are used to describe our Lord Jesus in Revelation 22:13. So now, we see these terms to describe in part who Jesus really is in His eternal nature and being.

- Alpha and Omega (1:8, 11).
- Beginning and Ending (1:8; 3:14).
- First and Last (1:11, 17; 2:8).
- Author and Finisher (Heb. 12:2).

With this in mind, where do we get the well-worn phrase: "The Second Person of the Trinity?" Nowhere in Sacred Writ do we ever find Jesus in "second place", nor is He ever referred to as being "second". Always, He declared Himself to be "equal with the Father" and "one" with Him. *"Let this mind be in you which was also in Christ Jesus: who being in the form of God, thought it not robbery to be equal with God"* (Phil. 2:5,6). *"I and My Father are one!"* (John 10:30).

There is no indication here that Jesus is anything less than equal to and one with His Heavenly Father. Let's not place Him in second place but totally one with the Triune Godhead. *"For in him dwelleth all the fullness of the Godhead bodily!"* (Col. 2:9).

Verses 9-11:

9. *I John, who also am your brother, and companion in tribulation, and in the kingdom and patience of Jesus Christ, was in the isle that is called Patmos, for the word of God, and for the testimony of Jesus Christ.*

10. *I was in the Spirit on the Lord's day, and heard behind me a great voice, as of a trumpet,*

11. *Saying, I am Alpha and Omega, the first and the last and, What thou seest, write in a book, and send it unto the seven churches which are in Asia: unto Ephesus, and unto Smyrna, and unto Pergamos, and unto Thyatira, and unto Sardis, and unto Philadelphia, and unto Laodicea.*

The tribulation referred to here in verse 9 is not the great and final tribulation recorded later in Revelation. It is rather a reference to John's suffering in exile on the Island of Patmos. He was in the Spirit on the Lord's Day that is the day of God's visitation to him with the apocalypse of the Lord Jesus Christ. He was caught up in the Spirit into the heavenlies where all these things were shown unto him.

In spite of the gloom of his circumstances, John was still in the Spirit, sensitive and receptive to the voice of the Word. Suddenly, behind him a great voice trumpeted into his ears. Why was this like a trumpet? We must not hurry past the little points of detail for they are all meaningful in the Word of God.

Since the Bible is its own interpreter, we can expect to find the explanation of the trumpet hidden in the Old Testament types and shadows or in the   New Testament fulfillment of the same. In this type we find the word sounding like a trumpet on Mount Sinai. *"When the trumpet soundeth long, they shall come up to the mount."* (Exodus 19:13).

The sounding of the trumpet symbolizes the voice of God speaking forth. In Moses' day, it was a call to Israel to come to the foot of the mountain for God was about to give them His law. The voice of the trumpet that spoke to John was similar to what happened to Moses and the people of Israel.

And it came to pass on the third day in the morning, that there were thunders and lightnings, and a thick cloud upon the mount, and the voice of the trumpet exceeding loud; so that all the people that was in the camp trembled.

(Exod.19:16)

The voice of the trumpet was the very voice of God! *"And when the trumpet sounded long, and waxed louder and louder, Moses spake, and God answered him by a voice."* (Exod.19:19).

The sound of the voice of God as a trumpet was really a call to worship. It was necessary to cause John to position himself in a state of humility, reverence and fear. This noise caught John's attention, opened his ears to hear the word of the Lord and loosened his tongue to speak. His experience with the voice of the trumpet caught his whole attention and caused him to turn and fall prostrate as a dead man at the feet of the exalted Christ. When Christ returns for His overcoming church, like John, the call will cause us to respond.

"For the Lord himself shall descend from heaven with a shout, with the voice of the archangel, and with the trump of God: and the dead in Christ shall rise first; then we which are alive and remain shall be caught up together with them in the clouds to meet the Lord in the air; and so shall we ever be with the Lord!" (I Thess. 4:16,17).

John heard the command of the Lord to write what he saw in a book. After that, there was the responsibility to send it forth. Thus he said, *"He that hath an ear, let him hear what the Spirit saith unto the churches."* The word of Revelation was to be sent to seven individual churches that existed in John's day, which represented the seven ages of the church from that day until now. The message to each church closes with a personal challenge. All seven messages have a spiritual challenge to all believers. Today's believer must walk in the challenge and the promise of all seven churches. We must take heed lest we make the same mistakes that were made by the church in the past ages. For example, what made the church at Ephesus die and pass away? Was it not that they *"left their first love"*? In turn, we are exhorted to watch and pray lest we also are tempted to leave our first love, the Lord Jesus Christ.

A sincere Bible student can readily see that the seven churches represent the whole 'Church Age' beginning with the Apostolic Church of Ephesus. They had all of the gifts, the fruit and the full stature of revealed truth given by Christ Himself. They had the full knowledge of salvation through the shed blood of Christ as well as water baptism in His name, His death and His life as it tells us in Romans 6:3-5.

The truth of the baptism of the Holy Spirit with the evidence of speaking in tongues was also the norm of the early church of the apostle's day. Most of these truths were lost through the years until the restoration of truth to the church of this end time.

The Early Church had the wisdom, knowledge and understanding of the Word of God as well as possessing the hidden manna of the mysteries of God. In writing to the church of Ephesus in his epistle, the Apostle Paul conveyed these mysteries and knowledge and shared the revelation of growing up into Jesus Christ. *"Till we all come in the unity of the faith, and of the knowledge of the Son of God, unto a perfect (mature) man, unto the measure of the stature of the fullness of Christ."* (Eph.

4:13).

When we were first saved and converted, we fell at the foot of the old rugged cross, at the feet of Jesus, to confess our sins and accept Him as our Lord and Savior. When we grew up a little more, we followed Him in water baptism continuing our growing up in Christ. As we grew more in love with Him, we did all we could to be in the realm of His heart. Then, as our striving was to grow up into His full stature, we finally endeavored to fulfill the words of the Apostle Paul in Philippians 2:5, *"Let this mind be in you, which was also in Christ Jesus!"*

THE DESCRIPTION OF JESUS

Verses 12-16:

12. *And I turned to see the voice that spake with me. And being turned, I saw seven golden candlesticks (lampstands)*

13. *And in the midst of the seven candlesticks one like unto the Son of man, clothed with a garment down to the foot, and girt about the paps (breast) with a golden girdle.*

14. *His head and his hairs were white like wool, as white as snow; and his eyes were as a flame of fire;*

15. *And his feet like unto fine brass, as if they burned in a furnace; and his voice as the sound of many waters.*

16. *And he had in his right hand seven stars: and out of his mouth went a sharp twoedged sword: and his countenance was as the sun shineth in his strength.*

Jesus was never described anywhere in the Bible like this. Only John had this awesome portrayal of Christ. Though He was young, yet His hair was white as snow like an aged man. Why? Because He was *"the Ancient of Days"* according to Daniel 7:22. His eyes were as a flame of fire because He is the all-seeing eye of the Father. His feet were like fine brass because they were the strong foundation of His church, which is His body. His countenance was as the sun to fulfill the Scripture, which declares, *"The sun of righteousness shall arise with healing in his wings."* (Mal.4:2). Thus we see the awesome beauty of the glorified Christ at the right hand of the Majesty on high.

In the great move of God in 1948, many wonderful songs and choruses were birthed as they are in every great revival. Among them was this chorus:

Behold, what manner of Man is this who stands
twixt God and man;
Whose eyes are as a flame of fire, whose fan is in His hand.
John saw Him midst the seven churches
as the Son in brilliancy;
Behold, what manner of Man is this,
what manner of Man is He!
He's the Lord of Glory, He is the Great I Am;
The Alpha and Omega, the beginning and the end.
His name is Wonderful, the Prince of Peace is He;
The Everlasting Father throughout eternity.

Verses 17-20:

17. *And when I saw him, I fell at his feet as dead. And he laid his right hand upon me, saying unto me, Fear not; I am the first and the last.*

18. *I am he that liveth, and was dead, and behold, I am alive forevermore. Amen; and have the keys of hell and of death.*

19. *Write these things which thou hast seen, and the things which are, and the things which shall be hereafter:*

20. *The mystery of the seven stars which thou sawest in my right hand, and the seven golden candlesticks The seven stars are the angels of the seven churches; and the seven candlesticks which thou sawest are the seven churches.*

The writer of Hebrews made this statement: *"It is a fearful thing to fall into the hands of the   living God!"* (Heb.10:31). John must have felt this *"fearful thing"* as he fell down in the Spirit as one dead in the presence of the Lord of Glory. Jesus told him, however, as He always did to His disciples while He was on earth with them, *"Fear not!"*

Now, Jesus declares these astounding words. *"I HAVE THE KEYS OF HELL AND OF DEATH!"* Remember, the last enemy that will be destroyed is death, as we will then have eternal life. When Jesus died on the cross, His spirit went back to the Father, His body went into the borrowed tomb of Joseph of Arimathea, but His soul went into hell (Hades). This is why the prophetic scriptures declared, *"For thou wilt not leave my soul in hell; neither wilt thou suffer thine Holy One to see corruption."* (Ps.16:10).

While in that place of the underworld, He conquered once and for all the satanic forces and took triumph over them. Ps. 24:7 to 10 reads like this:

"Lift up your heads, O ye gates; and be ye lift up, ye everlasting doors; and the King of Glory shall come in!
Who is this King of Glory? The Lord strong and mighty, the Lord mighty in battle (against Satan)."
Lift up your heads, O ye gates; even lift them up, ye everlasting doors; and the King of Glory shall come in!
Who is this King of Glory? The Lord of hosts, he is the King of Glory. Selah!"

Jesus, during those three days prior to His glorious resurrection, went down into Hades and took from satan the keys of death and of hell. That is why in our text, He declared that He now has them. Beloved, satan has no rule over your future or your life. Those keys belong to the Lord Jesus Christ! Did you ever wonder why that old witch of Endor in First Samuel 28:7 could call up Samuel from the grave at the bidding of backslidden Saul? Because she had a familiar spirit and was of her father, the devil.

The enemy at that time had the keys of death and hell. Jesus has them now, so no fortune teller or soothsayer can bring back anyone from the beyond. The blessed promise is that we will be united with Jesus on that great Resurrection morning. Old Daddy Abbott, senior elder of our church in Michigan, always requested the old song from the hymnal, which gives us that wonderful hope of the Resurrection. We sang it on many great Sunday night evangelistic services. Today, it seems as if Sunday night services are a thing of the past.

In the great triumphant morning
When we hear the Bridegroom cry,
And the dead in Christ shall rise;
We'll be changed to life immortal
In the twinkling of an eye
And meet Jesus in the skies.
We shall all rise to meet Him;
We shall all go to greet Him
In the morning when the dead in Christ shall rise.
We shall all rise to meet Him;
We shall all go to greet Him,
We will have the marriage supper up in the skies.

A total of 18 "Sevens" are recorded in Revelation:

1. Churches	1:4,11; Chapters 2, 3
2. Spirits	1:4; 3:1; 4:5; 5:6
3. Candlesticks	1:12,13,20
4. Stars	1:16,20; 2:1; 3:1
5. Lamps	4:5
6. Seals	5:1,5
7. Horns	5:6
8. Eyes	5:6
9. Angels	8:2,6;15:1,6,8;16:1;17:1;21:9
10. Trumpets	8:2,6

11. Thunders	10:3,4
12. Thousand men	11:13
13. Heads	12:3; 13:1; 17:3-8
14. Crowns	12:3
15. Last plagues	15:1,6,8
16. Golden vials	15:7; 17:1; 21:9
17. Mountains	17:9
18. Kings/Kingdoms	17:10,11

THE ANGELS OF THE APOCALYPSE

Of all the Books of the Bible, the Book of Revelation has more to say about angels than any other. Besides the 'angels' of the Seven Churches, which are really the messengers to those churches, we have angels of many categories. There are angelic messengers. There are angels of judgment. There are warring angels. There are angels of proclamation, and the list goes on. Here are all the angels mentioned in the Apocalypse.

1:1 - Jesus' angel.

5:2 - Strong angel.

5:11 - Many angels.

7:1 - Four angels.

7:2 - Another angel.

8:2 - Seven trumpet angels.

8:13 - Flying angel.

9:11 - Angel, bottomless pit.

9:14 - Four river angels.

10:1 - Mighty angel.

14:6 - Gospel angel.

14:8 - Babylon angel.

14:9 - Warning angel.

14:15 - Temple angel.

14:17 - Temple angel II.

14:18 - Altar angel.

15:1 - Seven vial angels.

16:7 - Altar angel II.

18:1 - Glory angel.

18:21 - Mighty angel II.

19:17 - Sun angel.

20:1 - Angel, bottomless pit.

22:6 - Revealing angel.

22:8 - Revealing angel II.

CHAPTER 2

THE MESSAGE TO THE SEVEN CHURCHES

CHURCH	TIME	ANGEL	KIND
Ephesus	53-170	Paul	Foundational
Smyrna	170-312	Polycarp	Suffering
Pergamos	312-606	Martin	Tolerant
Thyatira	606-1517	Columba	Compromising
Sardis	1517-1750	Luther	Reviving
Philadelphia	1750-1975	Wesley	Restoring
Laodicea	1975-End	Prophets	Lukewarm

EPHESUS
The Foundational Church

Revelation 2:1-7:

1. Unto the angel of the church of Ephesus write: These things saith he that holdeth the seven stars in his right hand, who walketh in the midst of the seven golden candlesticks;

2. I know thy works, and thy labour, and thy patience, and how thou canst not bear them which are evil; and thou hast tried them which say they are apostles and are not, and hast found them liars:

3. And hast borne, and hast patience, and for my name's sake hast laboured, and hast not fainted.

4. Nevertheless I have somewhat against thee, because thou hast left thy first love.

5. Remember therefore from whence thou art fallen, and repent, and do the first works, or else I will come unto thee quickly, and will remove thy candlestick out of his place, except thou repent.
6. But this thou hast, that thou hatest the deeds of the Nicolaitans, which I also hate.
7. He that hath an ear, let him hear what the Spirit saith unto the churches; To him that overcometh will I give to eat of the tree of life, which is in the midst of the paradise of God.

THE ANGEL/MESSENGER OF EPHESUS

The great Apostle Paul, the one *"born out of due time"* according to his own testimony given in I Corinthians 15:8, was undoubtedly the angel/messenger of the Church of Ephesus. He was the founder of the church and taught them and established them in the new found Christian faith.

Paul withstood the false teachings of the day as well as the cult of Diana, which was rampant in Ephesus. Paul's teaching in that day concerning women in the church was brought on because of the women followers of this cult. It is unfortunate that so many male teachers in the church today still want to enforce something that was written for that time and place.

The very same Apostle Paul also wrote these words to balance his teaching, *For ye are all the children of God by faith in Christ Jesus...There is neither Jew nor Greek, there is neither bond nor free, there is neither male or female; for ye are all one in Christ Jesus!* (Gal. 3:26,28).

Paul later appointed his son in the gospel, Timothy, as the Bishop of the Ephesus Church and it is interesting to note that the very writer of Revelation, the Apostle John, spent his final days on earth at Ephesus.

FACTS ABOUT EPHESUS

Ephesus was a key city in the Province of Asia Minor. Several major roads converged there. Paul spent three years ministering there. It was the seat of the Temple of Diana, which was one of the Seven Wonders of the Ancient World.

Ephesus means *"desirable"*. It was the first church era of the Seven Church Periods. The Lord Jesus walks in the midst of all His churches and holds His servants in His hands.

The Early Church was walking in separation from the world. The word "church" in Greek is *"ekklesia"*.[1] It means *"a called out company"*. The early church of Ephesus did not want just numbers at the expense of holy living. They were willing to endure persecution for the sake of the Gospel of Christ.

Still, DECLINE CAME! Decline has come to each Church Age. We are admonished by the Lord to return to our *"first love"* which the Lord says we *"left"*, not lost. It is one thing to lose something we love. It is another thing to just walk away and leave it.

Thus saith the Lord, I remember thee, the kindness of thy youth, the love of thine espousals when thou wentest after me in the wilderness, in a land that was not sown. Israel was holiness unto the Lord, the firstfruits of his increase.

(Jer. 2:1,2)

The place of Ephesus was quenched, their light put out. Today the city lies in ruins. It behooves us to live in the light of this example and walk in the prophetic promise to the overcomers.

---

[1] (Strong's #1577).

SATAN IS AT WORK

Beginning with the Church of Ephesus, we see the enemy, satan, at work among God's people. He is shown in the Book of Revelation, which we now study, in four forms of power as found in Revelation 20:2: satan, the devil, the serpent, and the great dragon.

In Revelation 12, he appears as a *"great red dragon"* and again in chapter 13 as a *"beast having seven heads and ten horns"*. He is none other than old Lucifer, the archenemy of the Church of the Lord Jesus Christ. He has always desired to "blaspheme" against the Lord and His Church. The blasphemous seven heads are these, which we will discuss more in Chapter 13.

1. THE HEAD OF DECEIT
2. THE HEAD OF AFFLICTION
3. THE HEAD OF BLASPHEMY
4. THE HEAD OF ENCHANTMENT
5. THE HEAD OF DEATH
6. THE HEAD OF IGNORANCE
7. THE HEAD OF REBELLION

Satan deceived the Ephesians to relax and count their works more important than their *"first love"*, the Lord Himself. The emphasis of the Book of Ephesians is *the believer's position in Christ!* It is not works; it is our position in Him. While Paul strongly opposed the idolatry that tried to come into the church through the idolatrous worship of the goddess Diana, John opposed the doctrine of one Nestorius who denied the incarnation of Christ saying that Christ was God-inspired but NOT God-made. That old doctrine is still around today in many of our modern churches who deny the true deity of our Lord Jesus.

Paul's farewell message to the saints at Ephesus included this challenge:

Take heed therefore unto yourselves and to all the flock over which the Holy Ghost hath made you overseers, to feed the church of God which he hath purchased with his own blood. For I know this, that after my departing shall grievious wolves enter in among you, not sparing the flock. Also of your own selves shall men arise, speaking perverse things, to draw away disciples after them.

(Acts 20:28-30)

JESUS COMMENDS THE CHURCH

1. For their works, their labors, their patience and their endurance.
2. Their stand against evil and their rejection of false apostles.
3. Their hate for the deeds of the Nicolaitanes.

There were three things in the Seven Churches that the Lord Jesus could not tolerate:
    1. The deeds of the Nicolaitanes.
    2. The Doctrine of Balaam.
    3. The spirit of Jezebel.

These three were truly the devil's trinity.

1. Nicolaitanes

What begins as *"the deeds of the Nicolaitanes"* (2:6) soon becomes *"the doctrine of the Nicolaitanes"* (2:15). In the Ephesus church the Nicolaitanes had an adverse effect and the Lord Jesus said He hated their *"deeds"*. They tried to conquer the laity. It was the earliest form of a priestly order that later divided the church into clergy and laity.

They taught impure doctrines such as having community wives which created adultery and fornication as well as eating foods offered unto idols. Ephesus had light and truth but somehow allowed satan's priests to become mixed in.

All their works they do for to be seen of men...And love the uppermost rooms at feasts, and the chief seats in the synagogues...and to be called of men, Rabbi, Rabbi. But be ye not called Rabbi for one is your Master, even Christ, and ye are all brethren. And call no man your father upon the earth, for one is your Father which is in heaven. Neither be ye called masters for one is your Master, even Christ. But he that is greatest among you shall be your servant.

(Matt. 23:5-11)

Christ's teaching about these fancy titles given by men to ministries is certainly quite clear from this Scripture. In this day of every preacher bearing some kind of fancy title, let us beware lest we allow ourselves to get into this kind of thing. It is enough just to be called "brother" or "sister" or "pastor" or "preacher".

Look at what the Early Church fathers had to say about the Nicolaitanes:

Ignatius: "Flee the impure Nicolaitanes who are lovers of pleasure and given to slanderous speeches. They affirm that unlawful unions are a good thing and place the highest happiness in worldly pleasures."

Irenaeus: "The Nicolaitanes were the followers of Nicolas one of the first seven ordained deacons. They lead lives of unrestrained indulgence. They teach it as a matter of indifference to practice adultery and to eat things sacrificed to idols."

Tertullian: "Nicolas was in the habit of indifference of both life and food. His followers constantly gave insult to the Holy

Ghost. He taught there were born demons and gods and spirits therefore mixtures made life happy and full and brought contentment, endeavoring to rule the laity with their doctrines."

2. Doctrine of Balaam

This doctrine was a mixture of worldliness, curses and condemnation. Balaam truly loved the wages of unrighteousness.

"Which have forsaken the right way, and are gone astray, following the way of Balaam...who loved the wages of unrighteousness." (2 Pet.2:15).

He desired to keep the people under condemnation which brings oppression. This was happening in the Church of Pergamos. Balaam counseled the Israelites to trespass against the Lord for the women of Moab to lay with the men of Israel. The Israelites joined with Baal-peor and ate the food offered to idols. The plague that followed cost Israel 24,000 lives who died in the judgment of God. (See Numbers 22.)

3. Spirit of Jezebel

Jezebel was the wife of King Ahab who was an evil king in the sight of the Lord. He did more to provoke God than any other king of Israel. (1 Kings 16:30,31). Jezebel was a killer of God's prophets. (1 Kings 18:4 & 19:2). In First Kings 21, this wicked woman had righteous Naboth put to death.

Jezebel took the money of Israel and erected two huge houses of worship to false gods Astarte and Baal. She forced herself and her evil ways upon the people. She seduced the servants of God to commit fornication. This evil spirit of Jezebel still roams the earth to seduce the servants of God as our text so clearly tells us.

"...that woman Jezebel, which calleth herself a prophetess, to teach and seduce my servants to commit fornication, and to eat things sacrificed unto idols."

Our hearts are grieved so many times these days to see great ministries diminished and destroyed because of this "Spirit of Jezebel" which seems so rampant in these last days. Pray always to overcome this spirit that is so prevalent in the earth.

THE PROMISE TO THE OVERCOMERS

"He that hath an ear, let him hear what the Spirit saith unto the churches; To him that overcometh will I give to eat of the tree of life which is in the midst of the paradise of God." (Rev. 2:7).

Three distinct places we find the *TREE OF LIFE:*

1. IN THE GARDEN OF EDEN

"And the Lord God planted a garden eastward in Eden, and there he put the man whom he has formed. And out of the ground made the Lord God to grow every tree that is pleasant to the sight and good for food; the TREE OF LIFE also in the midst of the garden." (Genesis 2:8,9).

2. IN THE WISDOM OF PROVERBS

"She is a TREE OF LIFE to them that lay hold on her (wisdom)." (Prov. 3:18).

"The fruit of righteousness is a TREE OF LIFE." (Prov. 11:30).

3. IN THE HOLY CITY OF GOD

"In the midst of the street of it and on either side of the river was there the TREE OF LIFE which bare twelve manner of fruits, and yielded her fruit every month; and the leaves of the TREE were for the healing of the nations." (Rev. 22:1,2).

SMYRNA
The Suffering Church

Revelation 2:8-11:

8. *And unto the angel of the church in Smyrna write; These things saith the First and the Last, which was dead, and is alive;*
9. *I know thy works, and tribulation, and poverty (but thou art rich) and I know the blasphemy of them which say they are Jews, and are not, but are of the synagogue of Satan.*
10. *Fear none of those things which thou shalt suffer; behold, the devil shall cast some of you into prison that ye may be tried; and ye shall have tribulation ten days; be thou faithful unto death, and I will give thee a crown of life.*
11. *He that hath an ear, let him hear what the Spirit saith unto the churches; He that overcometh shall not be hurt of the second death.*

FACTS ABOUT SMYRNA

Smyrna was an important port city in its day. The modern name for that city today is Izmir. The name Smyrna means *"myrrh; bitter"* and carries the meaning of suffering. Myrrh had to be crushed in order to bring out its fragrance. You will remember that myrrh was one of the gifts that was brought to the Christ child by the Wise Men from the east. During this period of time, shall we see the crushing of the Smyrna Church under the cruel heel of Pagan Rome. For years, there was constant martyrdom during this period. Though the Smyrna Church was in great tribulation and poverty, they were rich, not in this world's goods, but in faith and obedience.

This was one of the worst periods of persecution during which the early Christians were thrown to the lions. It is written about in the classic "Foxes Book of Martyrs". Thank God, those days were *"shortened for the elect's sake!"* During this time, the church grew and established many of the 'Doctrines of the Faith' that have remained unto this day.

THE ANGEL/MESSENGER OF SMYRNA

The early church father, Polycarp, is considered to be the angel or messenger of the church of Smyrna.

After the martyrdom of Polycarp, another church father, Irenaeus, took the leadership role. Polycarp was a great man who lived a most blameless life and was very close to the Lord Jesus. He had many followers including the disciple Irenaeus. He was too old to flee so surrendered to Rome. He asked for and was granted permission to pray two hours for his brethren in the Lord, his enemies and his cruel captors. He stood firm, refusing to deny his Lord. He was placed at the stake with his hands untied at his own request. The fire was lit, but it bent away from his body refusing to touch him. He was then pierced through with the sword. As this was being done, water gushed forth from his side and drowned out the flames. His spirit was actually seen to depart in the form of a white dove released from his bosom.

Irenaeus, who followed Polycarp, was exalted by the Lord and filled with the Holy Ghost. He taught about the Lord with clarity and with power. He had wonderful understanding and great leadership.

THE COMMENDATION OF SMYRNA

1. *"I know your WORKS, and TRIBULATION, and POVERTY (but you are really RICH)"*

    They may have been poor in this world, but they were rich in eternal values.

2. Jesus commended them for standing up against false teachers who had crept into the church. *"They say they are Jews (believers) but are not!"*

3. The Lord encouraged them not to fear the things they would suffer for His namesake. Some would be cast into prison and others would have great trials for ten days.

The number ten is a legal number under the law. They were tried for ten years under the cruel hand of the Emperor Diocletion, the most wicked of all the Roman Emperors. This was from A.D. 302 until A.D. 312 when God put His servant Constantine on the throne of Rome and the terrible persecution was finally brought to a close. It also brought about a great mixture of the world into the church.

THE PROMISE TO THE OVERCOMERS

"Be thou faithful unto death, and I will give thee a crown of life!"

"He that overcometh shall not be hurt of the second death."

What wonderful promises to a church that had gone through so much suffering and persecution. Even today, God has a *"martyr's crown"* for those who are faithful unto death in their calling. Many years ago, in the Belgian Congo, Africa there was a horrible uprising of the natives who called themselves "simbas", a word taken from the Swahili word for lion. They stormed the nation driving out the whites and slaughtering many. Many missionaries were beheaded for the sake of the gospel, refusing to leave the post to which God has called them. Rev. Tucker of the Assemblies of God was one of those brave martyrs, as was the co-worker of my own brother, Harold Salseth. Harold and his family escaped only by a miracle as they fled the oncoming "simbas". They escaped with only the clothes on their backs as they fled toward a nearby river. Arriving at the river, they found God had provided a couple of dugout canoes into which they climbed and floated down stream and away from certain death.

In another instance in our own ministry, we witnessed the martyrdom of a precious Bible School student who trained under us in the Philippine Islands. Our team had gone high up in the mountains of Northern Luzon to preach the gospel. Many natives were converted to the Lord and Pastor Efren, our student, was staying behind to teach them and head up the newly planted church. That Sunday afternoon he took a large group of converts down to the Abra River to be baptized in water. Following the service, he sat on a rock by the riverside to meditate and pray. Suddenly, a shot rang out and he fell over dead, his blood flowing into the water. The enemy was angered over so many of his followers being converted to the Lord Jesus Christ. We brought his body back down to the Bible School for burial and he has been remembered to this day as a brave martyr, the first of such from Miracle Bible College.

"Not hurt of the second death" was the overcomer's promise. The *Second Death* is referred to in Revelation 20:6 where the Scripture declares, *"Blessed and holy is he that hath part in the first resurrection; on such the <u>second death</u> hath no power!"*

Again in Revelation 20:14 & 15 the Word of God says, *"And death and hell were cast into the lake of fire, and whosoever was not found written in the Book of Life was cast into the lake of fire. <u>This is the second death</u>*

No believer should ever experience the *Second Death*. Our sins have already been judged at Calvary through our Lord Jesus Christ. We will not be judged at the Great White Throne Judgment, but our works will be judged at the Judgment Seat of Christ to see whether they will be gold, silver and precious stones or wood, hay and stubble. Let us take heed that we build upon a sure foundation for the works that we may do so that they will stand in the Day of Judgment.

"For other foundation can no man lay than that is laid, which is Jesus Christ. Now if any man build upon this foundation gold, silver, precious stones, (or) wood, hay, stubble; Every man's work shall be made manifest for the day shall declare

it, because it shall be revealed by fire; and the fire shall try every man's work of what sort it is. If any man's work abide which he hath built thereupon, he shall receive a reward. If any man's work shall be burned, he shall suffer loss; but he himself shall be saved, yet so as by fire"

(1 Cor.3:11-15)

PERGAMOS
The Tolerant Church

Revelation 2:12-17:

12. *And to the angel of the church in Pergamos write: These things saith he which hath the sharp sword with two edges;*

13. *I know thy works, and where thou dwellest, even where Satan's seat is; and thou holdest fast my name, and hast not denied my faith, even in those days wherein Antipas was my faithful martyr, who was slain among you, where Satan dwelleth.*

14. *But I have a few things against thee because thou hast there them that hold the doctrine of Balaam, who taught Balac to cast a stumblingblock before the children of Israel to eat things sacrificed unto idols, and to commit fornication.*

15. *So hast thou also them that hold the doctrine of the Nicolaitanes, which thing I hate.*

16. *Repent; or else I will come unto thee quickly, and I will fight against them with the sword of my mouth.*

17. *He that hath an ear, let him hear what the Spirit saith unto the churches; To him that overcometh will I give to eat of the hidden manna, and will give him a white stone, and in the stone a new name written, which no man knoweth saving he that receiveth it.*

FACTS ABOUT PERGAMOS

Pergamos was an important city about 15 miles from the sea. This city was the first center of emperor worship in Asia Minor. In the days of John, it was the Roman capitol of Asia. It was the source of the fashions of that day. It was a city of luxurious pagan temples, but there was also a thriving Christian assembly of believers in Pergamos.

The name Pergamos has two meanings. The first is *"marriage"*; the second is *"elevated"*. This depicts a time when the church and state were *married* and joined under Constantine the Great. It also depicts the time when the church was *elevated* to a place of power in Rome, but alas became married to the world. No wonder that the Pergamos church was considered to be "The Tolerant Church."

After the death of the cruel Roman Emperor, Diocletian, Constantine claimed to have a vision of a "Cross of Fire" in the sky. He heard a voice telling him "by this sign you will conquer". He called in all of the Christian bishops to understand better the doctrines of Christendom. He declared himself to be God's candidate and protector and thus became the first Christian Emperor of the world. He was crowned up in York, England, which was a part of the vast Roman Empire of that day. His very first act was to stop all persecution of Christians in the world. He bestowed honors upon all the bishops making them leaders.

The people, especially the Christians who had so looked for Christ's Kingdom to come in the midst of their dreadful persecutions, declared, "We have been looking for Christ to come and reign, but we have been wrong. Constantine's empire IS Christ's Kingdom!"

So were the church and state married as one – The Roman Empire and the Roman Catholic Church!

THE ANGEL/MESSENGER OF PERGAMOS

The angel or messenger of this Church Age was a man named St. Martin of Tours who was born in A.D. 315 in Hungary. His life work was, however, in France in and around Tours. He died in A.D. 399. His ministry was most like that of the great Apostle Paul. It is interesting to note that he was the uncle of St. Patrick of Ireland. None of these great early church "saints" were ever really Roman Catholic, as we would consider that church today. They were all a part of the universal church of that period of time.

Martin was converted to Christ while he was following a career as a professional soldier. It was while he was still engaged in this occupation that a most remarkable miracle occurred. It is recorded that a beggar lay sick in the streets of the town where Martin was posted. The winter cold was more than he could bear, as he was so poorly clothed. No one paid any attention to his desperate need until one day Martin came along. Seeing the poor man's plight, but not having an extra garment, he took off his cloak, cut it in two with his sword, and wrapped it around the freezing man. That very night the Lord Jesus appeared to him a vision. There Jesus stood, like a beggar, wrapped in half of Martin's garment. Jesus spoke to him and said "Martin, you have clothed Me with your garment!" From that time on, Martin served the Lord with all his heart and his life became a series of miracles.

Martin took a very adamant stand against idolatry. He cut down the groves, broke up the images and pulled down the pagan altars. He was confronted by the pagans many times and would challenge them even as did Elijah with the prophets of Baal. Once he offered to be tied to a tree on its underside so that when it was cut down it would surely crush him to death. The wily heathen tied him to a tree growing on the side of a hill, knowing that when they cut it down it would surely fall downhill with the pull of gravity. Just as the tree began to fall, God turned it around and it fell uphill contrary to all the laws of nature. The fleeing heathen were crushed as the tree fell on many of them. History records that at least three times God used Martin to raise the dead. He truly deserved to be called "The angel of the Church of Pergamos".

THE COMMENDATION OF PERGAMOS

As in the other churches of Asia, Jesus first commends before he condemns. Here is the commendation of this third of the seven churches.

1. I know your works (assuming that they were good).
2. I know the hard place wherein you dwell (where satan's seat is).
3. You have held fast to My name!
4. You have not denied My faith!
5. You have even borne up under martyrdom (of My servant Antipas).

Good works in the name of the Lord are very important for the church and for the individual Christian. We do not do good works, as some religious people do, to earn God's favor or to make up for bad things we have done as some form of penance. We work for our Lord Jesus because we love Him and want to see His Kingdom flourish upon the earth. For years, we have sung this little chorus out of our hearts:

> We'll work 'til Jesus comes;
> We'll work 'til Jesus comes;
> We'll work 'til Jesus comes,
> Then we'll be gathered home!

Our own personal work may soon be done on this earth as we are in our eighties now, but we know that our reward is awaiting us at His judgment seat. The greatest reward any of us can achieve is just to be at the feet of Jesus and hear Him say, *"Well done, thou good and faithful servant, enter thou in to the joys of the Lord!"*

Some of us dwell in a more difficult place than others. This seems to be our lot in life. We have learned that we can bloom where we are planted. This church of Pergamos dwelt in a very hard place, but they prospered and spread the glorious gospel throughout that region of the then known world. We can surely do the same where God has planted us. We have been in the ministry all our lives since teenagers. We pastored our first church at age 19. We didn't know very much, but God was good to send us people that didn't know much either so we all learned together. It seems we always pastored in small towns and out of the way places. We never had mega-churches, but God always gave us souls and our churches grew and bloomed where they were planted.

Under the leading and the direction of the Lord, He used us to pioneer and minister in churches in the following locations in the U.S. along with scores of others in the nations of the world.

1949 – Wilson Community Church, Wilson, WI
1951 – First Assembly of God, Waupaca, WI
1957 – Gospel Tabernacle, Rice Lake, WI
1964 – Pleasant Plain Gospel Church, Cameron, WI
1969 – Christian Fellowship, Centuria, WI
1970 – Christian Center, Grand Forks, ND
1972 – Liberty Christian Center, Duluth, MN
1974 – Christian Fellowship Center, Brighton, MI

Christ's third commendation of Pergamos was that they held fast to His Name. We sing so much about His Name; we preach so much about His Name; we do so many of our Christian works in His Name, so we must never give into this modern trend of just using the name of God without ever saying what it is. Allah is certainly not His Name, even though we are led to believe the lie that Allah is the same God as Jehovah. Yahweh is not His Name, even though it is a good Hebrew word for God. The Scriptures are very clear as to His Name.

"For there is none other <u>Name</u> under heaven given among men whereby we must be saved!" (Acts 4:12).

"Therefore let all the house of Israel know assuredly, that God (the Father) hath made <u>that same JESUS</u>, whom ye have crucified, both <u>LORD and CHRIST!</u>" (Acts 2:37).

This should be plain enough to see that the Eternal Godhead has given a 'NAME' whereby He does His eternal business on this earth. That name is 'THE LORD JESUS CHRIST'. The Pergamos Church did *"not deny His Name"*. Let us make sure that our church today does not deny His Name either.

"You have not denied My faith!" was the fourth commendation Christ gave to this church. We know that the Word of God declares in Hebrews 11:6, *"But <u>without faith</u> it is impossible to please God!"*

The Pergamos Church never denied their faith even though they dwelt in a hard place. It seems that the very seat of satan was in the place where this early church was established. It is sometimes hard to have faith when we are in such a difficult place. We have found through our years of ministry in over sixty nations of the world, that many places are much harder than others. Ancient religions, especially, block the move of the Spirit of God. Heathen customs, also, hinder the preaching of the gospel. Yet, we must still be bold in declaring our faith wherever and whenever we can. Jesus let us clearly know in Matthew 10:33, *"But whosoever shall deny Me before men, him will I also deny before My Father which is in heaven."*

Our son, Tim, was preaching in a heathen village over in South India with one of the national pastors. When he gave an invitation to accept Christ, some forty people came forward. This was an all-heathen village without a single believer in Christ. He challenged them to follow the Lord from then on and serve Him with all their hearts. The question was then asked Tim of those converts, "But where will we worship this Jesus? We have no church!" What else could we do? We built them a lovely concrete church building through the ministry of 'Christ for India' under the leadership of the late Dr. P.J. Titus and, at last report, it was packed to capacity with Christian believers in an all-heathen village, formerly that is. We cannot deny the faith of Christ and expect to prosper.

"This gospel of the Kingdom shall be preached in all the world for a witness unto all nations; and then shall the end come!" (Matt.24:14).

Matthew 24:14 has been called "The Mandate of the Church". Christ has promised us that He will return, but we must do our part to hasten that day by fulfilling the command of this Scripture.

Stand up, stand up for Jesus,
Ye soldiers of the cross!
Lift high His royal banner;
It must not suffer loss.
From victory unto victory
His army shall He lead.
'Till every foe is vanquished,
And Christ is Lord indeed!

'A FEW THINGS AGAINST THEE'

As in most of the Seven Churches, with the exception of Smyrna and Philadelphia, the Lord gives a rebuke for their failures, weaknesses and inconsistencies. Here in Pergamos they also had this condemnation to some in the church.

1. *"You hold the doctrine of Balaam"*
2. *"You hold the doctrine of the Nicolaitanes"*

We clearly defined these doctrines under the heading of the Church of Ephesus, but now they had crept over into this church as well. What was only the *"deeds of the Nicolaitanes"* in the Ephesus Church had now become an actual doctrine in the Pergamos church. If we let some little false teaching creep in as just a gentle suggestion, beware lest in due time it becomes a real doctrine of the church. Paul said in Ephesians 4:14, *"That we henceforth be no more children, tossed to and fro, and carried about with <u>every wind of doctrine!</u>"* (Emphasis added.)

The call of the Lord came to those who would not repent of these things that they would be fought against by the Lord *"with the sword of My mouth!"* The sword of His mouth is none other than His own precious Word, which is *"forever settled in heaven"* (Verse 16).

THE PROMISE TO THE OVERCOMERS

1. *"Hidden Manna"* - This is the promise of God's daily provision as it was for Israel's children.

Even more, it is the promise of the eternal bread of the revealed Word of God.

"Your fathers did eat <u>manna</u> in the wilderness and are dead. This is the <u>bread</u> which cometh down from heaven that a man may eat thereof, and not die. I am the living <u>bread (manna)</u> which came down from heaven. If any man eat of this <u>bread</u> he shall live forever!" (John 6: 49-51).

Jesus taught His disciples to pray, *"Give us this day our daily <u>bread!</u>"* This was to be more than just physical bread or daily sustenance for Jesus clearly taught us this: *"Man shall not live by bread alone, but by every word that proceedeth out of the mouth of God."* (Matt. 4:4).

The *"hidden manna"* is those wonderful precious truths that pop out at us from God's Word as we sincerely search for truth. In my own experience and that of my husband, we have read certain portions of the Bible scores of times, then suddenly one day it seems that a certain portion jumps out at us in Technicolor as if to say, "Look at this; it's been here all the time!" Why didn't we see it before? It seems in God's eternal plan that truth is revealed *"line upon line and precept upon precept!"* If He gave it to us all at once, we would not be able to take it and it would spiritually choke us.

Down through the ages, as we see them portrayed here in the Apocalypse, we see various Scriptural truths revealed in this unique way. Not all the truth we know today came in one big dose. We learned it little by little. Luther only knew *"justification by faith"*. He did not see water baptism by immersion or other later revealed truths. So it was down through the centuries of the Christian Church. Each era of time was given a new truth. At the beginning of the 20th Century, the truths of the Pentecostal Movement were revealed. They had been in the Word of God all the time, but now God was opening the eyes of the hungry to see them. The danger, of course, was that these truths would indeed become the final revelation of truth and everything would stop there. God still has wondrous truths to be revealed to His True Church now in this time and throughout eternity. Let us never stop hungering and thirsting for His righteousness and truth.

2. *"A White Stone"* - The white stone in that day was a verdict of an acquittal, not guilty—a black stone meant guilty and death. Jesus took our guilt on the cross of Calvary and made us *"free from the law of sin and death"*.

3.   *"A New Name Written"* – This new name would be given according to our new nature in Christ Jesus. The Prophet Isaiah declared it in 62:2, *"And thou shalt be called by a <u>new name</u> which the mouth of the Lord shall name."*

The gospel chorus we used to sing in church said,

> There's a new name written down in glory
> And it's mine, O yes, it's mine;
> And the white robed angels tell the story;
> A sinner has come home.
> There's a new name written down in glory
> And it's mine, O yes, it's mine.
> With my sins forgiven I am bound for heaven
> Never more to roam.

From our study of the Old Testament, we remember that God was in the name-changing business. God named the first woman on earth. He called her name Mrs. Adam in Genesis 5:2. Adam gave her the name Eve after the fall. God changed Abram to Abraham, the father of nations. He changed Sarai to Sarah, a mother of nations. He changed Jacob, the supplanter, to Israel, a prince with God. In the New Testament God changed Saul of Tarsus to Paul the great Apostle. He said to Simon Barjona, *"thou art Peter, and upon this rock I will build My Church!"* (Matt. 16:17). The church has called him Peter to this day.

Names in the Scripture describe 'nature' or the traits of our character. Nowhere is this more accurately portrayed than in the narrative of Jacob when he called his twelve sons before him at the time of his death and prophesied to each of them concerning their nature and future. This is described in detail in Genesis 49 and it is a most interesting study for the sincere Bible student.

When we as believers today accept the Lord Jesus, He in turn gives us a new nature. *"Behold, old things are passed away and all things become new!"* Our given names may stay the same, but praise God for the new name written up in glory!

THYATIRA
The Compromising Church

Revelation 2:18-29:

18. *And to the angel of the church in Thyatira write; These things saith the Son of God, who hath his eyes like unto a flame of fire, and his feet are like fine brass.*

19. *I know thy works, and charity, and service, and faith, and thy patience, and thy works; and the last to be more than the first.*

20. *Notwithstanding I have a few things against thee, because thou sufferest that woman Jezebel, which calleth herself a prophetess, to teach and to seduce my servants to commit fornication, and to eat things sacrificed to idols.*

21. *And I gave her space to repent of her fornication; and she repented not.*

22. *Behold, I will cast her into a bed, and them that commit adultery with her into great tribulation, except they repent of their deeds.*

23. *And I will kill her children with death; and all the churches shall know that I am he which searcheth the reins and hearts; and I will give unto every one of you according to your works.*

24. *But unto you I say, and unto the rest in Thyatira, as many as have not this doctrine, and which have not known the depths of Satan, as they speak; I will put upon you none other burden.*

25. *But that which ye have already hold fast till I come.*

26. *And he that overcometh, and keepeth my works unto the end, to him will I give power over the nations;*

27. *And he shall rule them with a rod of iron; as the vessels of a potter shall they be broken to shivers; even as I have received of my Father.*

28. *And I will give him the morning star.*

29. *He that hath an ear, let him hear what the Spirit saith unto the churches.*

FACTS ABOUT THYATIRA

Thyatira may have been the least important of the seven major cities of Asia Minor. It was some 40 miles southeast of Pergamos. Lydia, the seller of purple who opened her house to Paul in Acts 16:14, was from the city of Thyatira.

Thyatira has two different meanings: 1) *"A sacrifice"*; 2) *"Continually"*. From this, we may conclude "A continual sacrifice". During this period, the Catholic Church instituted the "continual sacrifice" in the mass as the papacy became more and more powerful. Thyatira covers the period of time that is often referred to as "The Dark Ages".

The "deeds" and "doctrine" of the Nicolaitanes affected the churches of Ephesus and Pergamos. The "doctrine" of Balaam affected the church of Pergamos as well. Now, the "spirit of Jezebel" affects the church of Thyatira. It is interesting to note that Jezebel was very adept in the art of mixing. She undertook to unite in one the true religion of Israel with the false religions of Phoenicia. The Romanism of the Dark Ages was a mixture as well. Many of the superstitions of heathenism and the occult were mixed with the practices and doctrines of Christianity during this period some of which have lasted even unto this day. God was not pleased with the mixture. If you watch DVD's, get one called "Ladyhawke" to show you just what I mean here by witchcraft and superstition being mixed into the Christian religion.

The main rebuke of the Lord to the Thyatira Church was that of their allowing the "spirit of Jezebel" to operate in their midst. Her teaching was seducing the servants of God to commit fornication and adultery. The spiritual meaning of this refers to the worship or union with idols, an illegal and immoral union.

THE ANGEL/MESSENGER OF THYATIRA

The angel or messenger of this church age was a mighty man of God from Great Britain named *Saint Columba*. He was born some sixty years after the death of another great man of God from the same area, namely St. Patrick. Contrary to common belief, neither Patrick nor Columba were ever Roman Catholic or even visited the city of Rome. Both were mightily used of God to work miracles and promote the gospel of Jesus Christ in England, Scotland and Ireland.

God called Columba in an audible voice to become His servant and a missionary to spread His Word. After this man heard God's voice, nothing could stop him from preaching and working miracles in the name of the Lord. Many historians acclaim him to be as one of the Apostolic Apostles. In one of his missionary journeys, he approached a walled city, common in those days, and found the gates barred against him. The heathen inside began to mock him with loud noises. Columba began to sing and his voice became so loud by the Spirit of God that he literally drowned out the noise of the heathen. Suddenly, of their own accord, the great city gates opened and the man of God entered and preached the gospel with signs and wonders.

In another instance, Columba entered a heathen city only to find the son of the chieftain was grievously ill. When the prayer of faith was prayed, the boy was instantly healed and the village was converted to Jesus. The pure uncompromising Word of God that Columba preached spread all across northern Europe and the message of Christianity gained mightily during this period even though it was called 'The Dark Ages'. No matter what the condition of the world, God always has a people who will glorify His name and not deny

His faith. Let us not forget that even in our day, God has a remnant who will not bow down to the modern teachings of the age, but will remain true to His Holy Word.

THE COMMENDATION OF THYATIRA

The Lord Jesus says to the saints in Thyatira that He knows several things about them and commends them.

1. *"Thy works"* – The fact that they were doing what Jesus had taught His early disciples to do brought His personal commendation.

    For I was hungred, and ye gave me meat; I was thirsty, and ye gave me drink; I was a stranger and ye took me in; Naked and ye clothed me; I was sick and ye visited me; I was in prison and ye came unto me ... Inasmuch as ye have done it unto one of the least of these my brethren, ye have done it unto me!

    (Matt. 25:35-40)

2. *"And charity"* – The same John who authored this Book of Revelation wrote in his first epistle these words:

    "Beloved, let us love one another for love is of God, and everyone that loveth is born of God and knoweth God!" (1 John 4:7).

3. *"And service"* - We do not serve God and do good works to earn salvation for it is a free gift of grace to all who believe. We do service for the Master because we are saved and desire to serve him out of a heart of love and appreciation for His matchless grace.

4. *"And faith"* - Jesus always looks on faith as a leading factor in receiving. So many times in His earthly ministry, He declared *"Go in peace, thy faith hath made thee whole!"* The church in Thyatira seemingly had this kind of faith even though it was in a period of works and religious spirits. God always has His own people no matter where or when. Let us strive to always be a part of that faith company that

pleases Him. *"Without faith it is impossible to please him!"* (Heb. 11:6).

5. *"And patience"* - Revelation 14:12 declares this, *"Here is the patience of the saints; here are they that keep the commandments of God, and the faith of Jesus!"*

The Apostle Paul tells us in Galatians that part of the Fruit of the Spirit is longsuffering or *patience.*

6. *"And thy works and the last to be more than the first."* Strange that God speaks of their works twice and says that the last are more than the first. Those first works were just described above, but what were the last ones? Look at what Jesus told His disciples to do and the early church followed what Christ had told them.

And when he had called unto him his twelve disciples, he gave them power against unclean spirits to cast them out, and to heal all manner of sickness and all manner of disease...And as ye go, preach saying, The Kingdom of Heaven is at hand. Heal the sick, cleanse the lepers, raise the dead, cast out devils; freely ye have received, freely give.

(Matt. 10:1,7,8)

The last works were the miracle works that Jesus commissioned His True Church to perform in His name. To us He gave this promise, *"Verily, verily, I say unto you, He that believeth on me, the works that I do shall he do also; and greater works than these shall he do, because I go unto my Father!"* (John 14:12).

A FEW THINGS AGAINST THEE

Once again, in His eternal wisdom, Jesus commands John to first commend the churches and then point out their weaknesses and failures that they might repent and become the overcomers that He desired them to be. Is it not the same today? Jesus wants all of us to be overcomers and inherit the promises that He has made to the overcomers.

To the Thyatira Church He declares that He had just a few things against them, primarily that they suffered the "spirit of Jezebel" to operate in their midst. We have learned by experience that this "spirit of Jezebel" can operate through women or men, as it is a seducing spirit that causes God's people to be unfaithful to the Lord and to His Church. It is not necessarily physical or sexual unfaithfulness that is involved in this spirit, but more times than not, it is unfaithfulness in the realm of the heart and soul, which causes those who belong to the Lord to be unfaithful to Him. Oh, that we would stand against that spirit that has captivated so many in the church in these last days.

Of course, there is the literal unfaithfulness, which the Jezebel spirit brings to the servants of God who are not constantly on guard. The two greatest things that seem to cause even great servants of God to fall are the same ones recorded in Revelation. The first is adultery and/or fornication. The second is unfaithfulness in the realm of finances. These are the two things that satan uses to trip up God's servants. We need only to look to the last few years to see how true this is and what reproach it has brought upon the Body of Christ. Let's be strong to stand against the "spirit of Jezebel" lest in a weak moment it attacks us when our guard is down.

HOLD FAST TILL I COME!

"I will put upon you none other burden, but that which ye have already. Hold fast till I come!"

Christ's coming was the hope of the early church. So much the more should it be *"the blessed hope"* of the church today. *"And that, knowing the time that now it is high time to awake out of sleep; for NOW is our salvation nearer than when we believed. The night is far spent, the day is at hand!"* (Rom. 13:11,12).

There are many who scoff today at the *"blessed hope"* or the *"catching away"* of God's overcoming saints before the wrath of God is poured out upon this old world. We still believe it and look forward to it even at our age. Whether we go by way of the undertaker or the upper-taker, we still hold on to that *"blessed hope"*. When we say goodbye to folks these days, we like to add "We'll see you here or there or in the air!"

> But until then my heart will go on singing;
> Until then with joy I'll carry on.
> Until that day my eyes behold that City;
> Until the day, God calls me home.

THE PROMISE TO THE OVERCOMERS

1. *"Power over the nations"*.
2. *"Rule them with a rod of iron"*.
3. *"I will give him the morning star"*.

These three wonderful promises belong to those who are overcomers. As we become overcomers in this life, we will become rulers with Him in eternity.

"And they lived and reigned with Christ a thousand years!" (Rev. 20:4).

The promise to the overcomers of receiving *"the morning star"* is the promise of the witness of the dawning of a new day. The Bible says that our Lord Jesus is *"the bright and morning star"*. What a joy to know that we will receive Him in all of His fullness and glory.

CHAPTER 3

THE MESSAGES TO THE CHURCHES CONTINUED

SARDIS
The Reviving Church

Revelation 3:1-6:

1. And unto the angel of the church in Sardis write; These things saith he that hath the seven Spirits of God, and the seven stars; I know thy works that thou hast a name that thou livest, and art dead.

2. Be watchful, and strengthen the things which remain, that are ready to die; for I have <u>not</u> found thy works perfect before God.

3. Remember therefore how thou hast received and heard, and hold fast and repent. If therefore thou shalt not watch, I will come on thee as a thief, and thou shalt not know what hour I will come unto thee.

4. Thou hast a few names even in Sardis which have not defiled their garments; and they shall walk with me in white for they are worthy.

5. He that overcometh, the same shall be clothed in white raiment; and I will not blot out his name out of the book of life, but I will confess his name before my Father, and before his angels.

6. He that hath an ear, let him hear what the Spirit saith unto the churches."

The Sardis Church period began with the Great Reformation spearheaded under Martin Luther. The years from 1517 A.D. to 1750 A.D., when John Wesley came on the scene, were considered the years of vast change in the religious world, as we shall see.

FACTS ABOUT SARDIS

Sardis was once a very proud and populous city in which the king, the richest man in the world at that time, had his royal residence. Nothing is left there today except historical ruins. The great Apostle Paul on one of his missionary journeys first preached the gospel in Sardis.

Sardis means *"a remnant"* or *"those who have escaped"*. This brings before us the great state churches of the Reformation period. They escaped as a remnant from the corruption of Rome only to fall at once into formalism and ritual themselves. While Martin Luther saw 'justification by faith' from the Scriptures, he looked no further to other great truths. Thus, it has been down through the ages so we must conclude that the revelation of truth is progressive. God must have planned it this way so that we would not spiritually choke on too much truth at one time.

THE ANGEL/MESSENGER OF SARDIS

The time had come for end to the formalism and ritual of the then existing church. It had drifted into every sort of perversion and the twisting of the Holy Word of God. Throughout the Dark Ages, God always had a special remnant of believers who followed wholly after Him and were not swayed by religion. Many of them, of course, were martyred for the gospel of Jesus Christ.

Even in the so-called "Dark Ages", God always had a group of *"come-outers"*. First, there were the 'Cathari' which means 'pure'. Following them came the 'Waldenses', followers of one Peter Waldo, a wealthy merchant from Lyon, France. These and others like them kept alive the true gospel message in spite of the backslidden church of those ages.

Now, God brings on the scene a Catholic priest who began to search the Scriptures that had been kept alive by being handwritten from generation to generation. With the invention by John Guttenburg of the printing press with moveable type, books could finally be printed by machine and not just handwritten. Thus the printing of the Bible was a marvelous part of the truth being placed in the hands of the people. This priest, *Martin Luther*, was undoubtedly the angel/messenger of this church age.

Luther was a brilliant scholar, studying to be a lawyer, when the death of a dear friend caused him to think of his own spiritual condition. He entered the Augustine convent at Erfurt, Germany in 1505 to study the Word of God. He did all he could to find peace with God through penance and church rituals, but could find none. He became a priest in the church, but still could find no peace with God. Then one day, God's Word struck home to his heart, *"The just shall live by faith!"* What a revelation! Finally, he came to the realization that all of his own works and righteousness was as *"filthy rags"*. Christ came into his heart and a new era in the earth was about to be birthed. The angel of the Sardis age was here!

Sauer's History of the Christian Church Volume 3 records this of Martin Luther: "Luther was a prophet, evangelist, speaker in tongues and interpreter in one person, endowed with all nine gifts of the Spirit." That's a lot to be said of one man.

Most everyone knows the story of October 31, 1517, the eve of All-Saints Day, now called "Halloween" meaning "Hallowed Evening". This was the evening in which Martin Luther posted his famous "95 Thesis" on the church door of the cathedral at Wittenburg, Germany. That day changed all of history and a new era for Jesus was born in the earth.

The Scriptures had already foretold that this day would come as we read Hebrews 9:8-11, *"The Holy Ghost this signifying that the way into the holiest of all was not yet made manifest, while as the first tabernacle was yet standing; Which was a figure for the time then present in which were offered both gifts and sacrifices, that could not make him that did the service perfect, as pertaining to the conscience; Which stood only in meats and drinks, and divers washings, and carnal ordinances imposed on them until the "TIME OF REFORMATION!"*

Could it be any plainer than this? While this Scripture was talking about Israel and all of the old customs and rituals, it certainly can rightly describe the church in Luther's day. He himself sought peace and forgiveness through the sacraments and rituals of the church and could not find it. Then came the *"TIME OF REFORMATION"* and everything changed. It's true, only JUSTIFICATION BY FAITH was revealed to Luther, but many other wonderful truths from God's Word were just over the horizon of a new day in the Church of the Lord Jesus Christ. Jesus himself had declared it, *"I will build MY CHURCH and the gates of hell shall not prevail against it!"* (Matt. 16:18).

Thank God, for Martin Luther and those who were to follow in the succession of producing 'His Glorious Church'.

NO REAL COMMENDATION OF SARDIS

Of all the Seven Churches of Asia, this church and that in Laodicea were the only ones to which our Lord gave no commendation as to their lives or works. This is quite a thing as there is nothing more encouraging for any church or individual than to hear the Almighty say, *"Well done thou good and faithful servant!"*

During this period of the church, vast congregations of people were 'baptized', literally sprinkled with water as in the tradition of the Roman Church and banded together taking the

Eucharist. Because of this newfound 'reformation', they were all zealous for the church, yet many of them were devoid of a personal experience with the Lord Jesus Christ.

The truth of being "born again" had not yet surfaced. It was largely for this reason that the Lord said to them these words, *"I know thy works that thou hast a name that thou livest and art dead!"* (3:1).

The same dead religious formality of the Roman Church of that day had now passed over to the followers of Luther even though he himself had a very personal experience with the Lord. The statement the Lord makes to Sardis, *"Be watchful and strengthen the things which remain!"* (3:2), refers to the fact that many were already drifting away from the Reformation truths.

What good is sound doctrine if it is only on paper in a statement of fundamental truth, but it is not written in our hearts by the Holy Spirit? It has been said that a man with an experience is never at the mercy of a man with a doctrine. This happened in the life of my husband when he was in his upper teens. He had met a group of young people who were a part of the Full Gospel Movement. He had never heard of such a thing so it was all totally new to him, but the blessing of God gripped his heart and he began to search for more of the Lord. One evening following a revival service in one of the churches, he was baptized in the Holy Spirit while driving his car home from the service. Being a part of a Reformation Church that had not gone beyond that truth, created quite a problem. Bob's mother called her pastor to come over and convince her son that this experience was not real. It was too late, of course, because he had already had the experience so, you see, it proves the saying.

THE CHALLENGE TO SARDIS

God graciously gives several things to challenge the Sardis Church to press on into Him.

1. *"Be watchful and strengthen the things which remain!"*

2. *"Remember therefore how thou hast received and heard!"*

3. *"Hold fast, and repent ... thou shalt not know what hour I will come upon thee!"*

Likewise, the Lord challenges us today because we are closer now to His return than ever before. While it is true as the Scripture says, *"No man knoweth the day nor the hour"*, yet we do know that *"the times and the seasons"* point to Christ's soon coming.

THE PROMISE TO THE OVERCOMERS

As in every church age and to every believer in the church, there is the promise of the Lord to those who were overcoming in that period of time. What our grandparents and parents had to overcome was much different than what we today must overcome. As our children grow up, they must overcome things that did not even exist in our day, and then, what about our grandchildren if Jesus tarries.

Each age seems to get progressively worse in some ways of the world, and yet, progressively better in knowledge and truth. The church today and the spreading of the gospel in this day are much more progressive than it was in the early days. What Daniel the Prophet saw in his vision of the endtimes, surely has come to pass in these last days, *"But thou, O Daniel, shut up the words, and seal the book, even to the time of the end; many shall run to and fro, and <u>knowledge shall be increased!</u>"* (Dan. 12:4, emphasis added).

God gave three promises to the Sardis overcomers and those in His Church who are overcoming in this day. The First Promise was this, *"He that overcometh the same shall be clothed in white raiment."*

In the Book of Revelation, three kinds of garments are given to those who will overcome in the realm that they are in. In each stage of spiritual life, there is an opportunity to overcome those things that would detract us from doing the will of God.

The garments given to overcomers are described in the Apocalypse as these: <u>White Robes</u> are given to the multitude of the redeemed who have made it into God's eternal Kingdom.

"After this I beheld, and lo, a great multitude, which no man could number, of all nations, and kindreds, and people, and tongues, stood before the throne, and before the Lamb, <u>clothed with white robes, and palms in their hands.</u>" (7:9, emphasis added).

<u>White Raiment</u> are garments given to those who, by their overcoming and spiritual growth, will be in a place of governmental leadership with Christ. *"And round about the throne were four and twenty seats; and upon the seats I saw four and twenty elders sitting, <u>clothed in white raiment,</u> and they had on their heads crowns of gold (rulership)."* (4:4, emphasis added).

<u>White Linen</u> is the dress for the Bride of Christ. *"Let us be glad and rejoice, and give honour unto him; for the marriage of the Lamb is come, and his wife hath made herself ready. And to her was granted that she should be <u>arrayed in fine linen, clean and white;</u> for the fine linen is the righteousness of saints."* (19:7,8, emphasis added).

The Second Promise to the Sardis overcomers: *"I will not blot out his name out of the Book of Life"*

As overcomers, we do have God's promise of His 'eternal security'. I am not speaking of a church doctrine, which may be warped out of context, but a true keeping by God's power if we want to be kept. *"Unto him who is able to keep you from falling and to present you faultless before the presence of his glory with exceeding joy!"* (Jude 24).

This is the promise to those who overcome *"by the blood of the Lamb and the word of their testimony."* Why would God even mention the idea of blotting out a person's name from His Eternal Book if we could never fall?

The Third Promise to the Sardis overcomers was this, *"I will confess his name before my Father and before his angels."* How wonderful to know that Jesus will confess us by name as His children before the eternal throne of God and before the myriads of angels of heaven. How blessed and privileged we are to be His children and heirs to His Eternal Kingdom.

PHILADELPHIA
The Restoring Church

Revelation 3:7-13:

7. *And unto the angel of the church in Philadelphia write; These things saith he that is holy, he that is true, he that hath the Key of David, he that openeth and no man shutteth, and shutteth and no man openeth;*

8. *I know thy works; behold I have set before thee an open door, and no man can shut it; for thou hast a little strength, and hast kept my word, and hast not denied my name.*

9. *Behold, I will make them of the synagogue of Satan, which say they are Jews, and are not, but do lie; behold, I will make them to come and worship before thy feet, and to know that I have loved thee.*

10. *Because thou hast kept the word of my patience, I also will keep thee from the hour of temptation (tribulation), which shall come upon all the world, to try them that dwell upon the earth.*

11. *Behold, I come quickly; hold that fast which thou hast, that no man take thy crown.*

12. *Him that overcometh will I make a pillar in the temple of my God, and he shall go no more out; and I will write upon him the name of my God, and the name of the city of my God, which is New Jerusalem, which cometh down out of heaven from my God; and I will write upon him my new name.*

13. *He that hath an ear, let him hear what the Spirit saith unto the churches.*

The Philadelphia period began with the coming to the church scene of John Wesley in about 1750. It lasted until approximately 1977 to 1980 according to our own experience of ministering during some of the Philadelphia Church age.

There is much thought concerning the ending of the Philadelphia age and the entering into the Laodicean Church age, as we shall share here. The Philadelphia age was the scene of restoration to the church and the great revivals of the 1800's and 1900's. What ended it and caused the church to enter into the "Luke-warm" age?

End-time church scholars have said that this age ended in 1906 when the Pentecostal Movement was birthed on Azuza Street in Los Angeles, California and spread rapidly around the world. They say this because every denomination of that day rejected in whole or in part this phenomenal move of the Holy Spirit which now has become the largest single force for God in the entire world. There is not a nation that has not been impacted in some way by the Pentecostal/Charismatic Movement.

The other scholars said that the Philadelphia age ended in 1948 when there was a paradigm shift in the earth which included the birth of the State of Israel as well as the birth of many great worldwide ministries. These ministries included such famous names as Billy Graham, Oral Roberts, T.L. Osborn, The Voice of Healing under Gordon Lindsay, Campus Crusade for Christ under Bill Bright and the list goes on and on. Our own ministry was birthed in 1948 as well.

Why would the age of "Brotherly Love" have ended in 1948? The thought was that the mighty "Latter Rain" revival, which compassed the whole, earth and began in 1948, was greatly rejected at that time as were many of the other ministries God raised up. Personally, these were some of the greatest years of our own ministry so we believe that these years were definitely part of the Philadelphia age.

The late great prophet, William Branham, whose name might be familiar to some of you, stated in his book on "The Seven Churches" that he believed that the end of the age of blessings would come in 1977. He clearly stated that he made this as a 'prediction' and not a 'prophecy'. He made such a prediction way back in the early thirties. Our own experience brings us to believe that somewhere between 1977 and 1980, the church world switched from Philadelphia to Laodicea.

I give you two reasons why this could be the period of time when the church made the shift along with the fact that the downhill slide had been going on for some long time already.

1. *David Wilkerson's Vision.*

This man of God, founder of Teen Challenge and Time's Square Church, spoke at the great Lutheran Charismatic Renewal Conference in the Minneapolis Auditorium on August 1, 1973. In his message to those hungry Lutheran and Catholic Charismatics, he declared his now famous vision given him by God in which he stated five things would happen in the next few years. Among these five things, which all have now come to pass, was the fact that the religious church would pull the 'red carpet' out from under the movement of the Holy Spirit. We were there that day in the front row of that great auditorium, as it were, by a miracle.

We had become quite involved in the stirring 'Charismatic Movement' especially that among the Lutherans and Catholics of Northern Wisconsin where we pastored for so many years. During that period, in the late sixties and early seventies, we saw scores of these denominational people receive the wonderful gift of the Holy Spirit with the evidence of "speaking in other tongues". Books on this move of God by such famous authors as John and Elizabeth Sherrill and Pat Boone only helped to stimulate and promote even further this mighty move of God among all of God's "frozen chosen".

My husband, Bob, was out in our garden picking green beans on that beautiful August day when, suddenly, God prompted him to come in the house and tell me that we were going immediately to Minneapolis to be in the Lutheran Conference on the Holy Spirit. I was not very excited about that long trip and, of all things, being in a Lutheran meeting. I had grown up among all Lutherans in our small Wisconsin town of Woodville, and their dry church never interested me at all. I was a fundamental Baptist and we were right that's all there was to that.

God had surely wanted us in that meeting, as it was the first time for David Wilkerson to unveil his vision and tell that vast congregation of some 12,000 people of that which was going to happen in the coming days. Among all else that was spoken, these words caused no little stir among the crowd, especially the religious ones who sat in black on that great platform. When Brother Wilkerson spoke these words, several of the Pharisees stomped off the platform in disgust and shook the dust off their feet. They seemed to be saying, "We are the scribes and we are the Pharisees and we won't stand for this!"

The stinging words of the prophecy were these: "The red carpet will soon be pulled out from under this mighty Charismatic move of the Holy Spirit!" He went on to say that the leaders of religion would fear for their kingdoms and try to pull the hungry and thirsty back into the fold of the old order of tradition. Well, it surely did happen and that mighty move of God we call "The Charismatic Movement" is almost non-existent as an entity. Most all of those who were brought into more of God during those days are now leaders and congregations of the Full Gospel and Free Churches of the Holy Spirit. Many of the mega-churches of today were birthed out of the Charismatic Movement.

2.   *The Word of God Community.*

In the spring of 1974, we moved to Brighton, Michigan where God used us to raise up a great Charismatic church in that community. It was a combination of Pentecostal, Charismatic and Word of Faith all rolled into one. People came, loved it, and became a part of it and to this day the church is still thriving. Shortly after arriving in Southeast Michigan, we heard of this move of the Holy Spirit taking place just sixteen miles down the road at the Word of God Community in Ann Arbor. This was known as the world's largest Charismatic Community. Through a series of circumstances, my husband was to find himself quite involved in what was happening there.

Derek Prince had been one of the speakers at the gatherings at Word of God and when a seeker had asked Dr. Prince about how to grow in God, he was advised to find a pastor who would baptize him in water by immersion. It was thus that a devout Catholic follower became a spirit-filled believer and a part of the Charismatic Movement. After this man was baptized, he invited my husband to start coming to their Thursday night gatherings at the large Catholic High School. Soon Bob was found on the inner circle and one of the men of God allowed to prophesy in the meetings. All of this was well and good and going along nicely until the "red carpet" was pulled out from under God's move just as David Wilkerson had prophesied.

A cardinal of the church was sent by his Holiness the Pope with a special message to the Community. While all of the work of the Holy Spirit was wonderful, the Pope of Rome was somewhat displeased that the Blessed Virgin was not uplifted in the meetings. Therefore, from henceforth a special "Hail, Mary" was to be said in every gathering. It was the last time my husband was ever in one of those gatherings. The "red carpet" had truly been snatched away!

With these two events transpiring, we were convinced that the Philadelphia age had come to a close and Laodicea had set finally set in.   The one redeeming feature of it all was the fact that God has always had a remnant of those who would not bow down to the golden idol of religion, who would not become lukewarm, who would always be a Philadelphian in spite of the spirit of the age. We believe and teach that God has a true *Philadelphia Church in a Laodicean Age!*

FACTS ABOUT PHILADELPHIA

The City of Philadelphia was located about 75 miles southeast of Sardis. It was the second largest city in Lydia and was built upon several hills in the famous wine-growing district. Though the city was subject to frequent earthquakes, it was in existence longer than any of the other seven cities of the Seven Churches. Today the city exists under the Turkish name of Alashehir, translated to mean "The City of God". Of course, it is known to mean "The City of Brotherly Love" taken from the Greek word for 'brotherly love', which is *phileo* from whence we derive Philadelphia. There are three Greek words to describe <u>love</u> in the New Testament times. The lowest form is *'eros'* from whence we get erotic or sexual love. The next is the one used here which we know as affectionate or brotherly love. The highest form is that wonderful word 'agape' speaking of God's love that he implants in us by His Holy Spirit.

It is interesting to note that for years one of the largest Pentecostal churches in the world was the famous "Filadelphia Church" in Stockholm, Sweden pastored by the late Dr. Lewi Pethrus. It influenced that nation and even had its own daily newspaper. The outreach ministry of that church spread to many nations and we preached in the "Filadelphia Church" in Argentina.

THE ANGEL/MESSENGER OF PHILADELPHIA

The messenger of this age was without a doubt John Wesley, the great reformer and founder of the Methodist Church. This great man of God was born in Epworth, England on June 17, 1703 and was one of nineteen children born to Samuel and Susanna Wesley. His father was a minister of the Church of England and, at the time of John's call into the ministry, was pastoring the Anglican Church on Aldersgate Street in London. Because of his 'revivalist' ways, John was put out of the church, but went across the street to the graveyard and started preaching from the top of a large tombstone. The crowds began coming and it was said in John Wesley's Journal, that "the slain on top of the ground were more than those under the ground."

John's personal conversion to Jesus Christ was attributed to the Moravian Brethren who, themselves, had experienced a mighty revival under the ministry of Count Zinzindorf of Austria. John had traveled with these anointed missionaries to the New World to preach in the colony of Georgia, but found he himself had not yet been converted. Through the zeal and faith of these Moravians, John Wesley was not only converted but was set on fire with the gospel message.

John Wesley set up a 'method' of spreading the gospel across Britain called "circuit riders", men who would ride their horses into communities and preach the gospel there. He was known to have ridden as much as 4,500 miles a year on horseback just to bring the glorious gospel to the lost. Though the Methodist Church was brought to pass through his efforts, he never had a desire to establish another denomination, but only to preach the gospel of his Lord and Savior. John Wesley died at the age of 88 having served God, as few men would even dare to think they might.

JESUS COMMENDATION TO THE PHILADELPHIA CHURCH

First, we must note that of all the churches, Christ had no condemnation for Philadelphia. We would all pray that our Lord would have no condemnation for us as well. That being said, let's look at how He commends this church which is an example of a true New Testament Church.

1. *"I know thy works!"*

   Once again, Jesus is implying by this statement that their works were righteous and approved by Him.

2. *"For thou hast a little strength"*

   In a time when perhaps many would have given up in their walk for Christ, He commended them for the strength that they did have. Jesus never condemns us when we are down or weak. He always encourages us to keep pressing on into Him. It is interesting to note that the word *'little'* used here does not mean just a tiny bit, but rather *"enough to do what God has called you to do!"*

3. *"And hast kept my word"*

There was no condemnation to the Philadelphia Church because they were based on the Word of God. We must always base all our beliefs and actions on what the Word of God declares and not on the current fads or movements of the day.

4. *"And hast not denied my name"*

This attribute is vital. We have sometimes been accused of being "Jesus Only" because of glorifying the name of Jesus so much in our meetings and in our worship and preaching. All we know is that the Scriptures declare, *"Neither is there salvation in any other; for there is none other name under heaven given among men, whereby we must be saved!"* (Acts 4:12).

A LOOK AT WHO IS SPEAKING

1. *"He that is holy!"* We would exhaust all possible pages and your valuable time if we even began to list all of the Scriptures which call our Lord 'holy'. We only know that we are admonished by His Word, *"But as he which hath called you is holy, so be ye holy in all manner of conversation; Because it is written, Be ye holy for I am holy!"* (1 Pet.1:15,16).

2. *"He that is true!"* When Jesus disciples asked Him about the way to heaven, He answered them, *"I am the way, the truth, and the life; no man cometh unto the Father but by me!"* (John 14:6).

3. *"He that hath the key of David!"* We know that keys are used to lock and unlock doors. Jesus gave the "Keys to the Kingdom" to Peter as a representative of believers and today we have those keys to open and shut through prayer. However, we must, ask, "What is this 'THE KEY OF DAVID'?

This passage here in Revelation 3 is really a quote from Isaiah 22:22 where the Word of God declares, *"And THE KEY OF THE HOUSE OF DAVID will I lay upon his shoulder, so that he shall open and none shall shut; and he shall shut and none shall open!"*

While this spoke at that time of Eliakim, the servant of the Lord and the treasurer of David's House, it is a prophetic word about our Lord Jesus Christ. Isaiah saw in his prophetic vision of the coming of Christ who He really was to be and declared it clearly in Isaiah 9:6, *"For unto us a child is born, unto us a son is given; and the government shall be upon his shoulder; and his name shall be called Wonderful, Counsellor, The Mighty God, The Everlasting Father, The Prince of Peace!"*

The Key of David is really the Key of our Lord Jesus as He said these words Himself in Revelation 22:16, *"I am the root and the offspring of David, and the bright and morning star!"*

THE KEY OF DAVID – A WORSHIPPER

David was a worshipper. That is all he knew how to do as he tended his father's flocks. Through this praise and worship, David conquered a lion and a bear and, ultimately, a giant who dared to defy the Living God. Our wonderful Biblical songbook, The Psalms, were written by David and his musicians. We have found in our meetings throughout all these many years, that more has happened in true worship and praise than one can imagine. Long before we ever gave an 'altar call', people were saved and healed and filled with the Holy Spirit all through our awesome praise and worship time in the services.

4. *"He that openeth, and no man shutteth; and shutteth and no man openeth!* We try so many times to open our own doors to the things in life. We have learned, sometimes the hard way, that the only doors that God wants us to enter into are the ones that He has opened for us. God's promise to the Philadelphia believers even in the church today is this wonderful promise, *"Behold, I have set before thee an open door, and no man can shut it!"*

SOME SPECIAL PROMISES TO THIS CHURCH

1. *Your enemies will come and worship at your feet.*

    This literally happened in our ministry many years ago. A neighboring pastor, whom we had baptized in water along with his whole family, later became very jealous of the growth of our church. He began to circulate all kinds of terrible rumors about us and even had our phones tapped to try to get something on us. Then one day he had a terrible accident and killed a little boy. It was not his fault as the child ran out in the road right in front of his car.

    Satan played on this man's mind as he had several children of his own. Finally, he could get no peace and one day appeared at our office door. He literally crawled up to my husband's feet on his hands and knees, begging forgiveness for the wrong he had done and ask for prayer to deliver him of the torment of this terrible tragedy. Of course, we had long since forgiven him and prayed earnestly for him.

2. *Those around will know that God loves you.*

    God does show special favor on those that He has called and chosen for His glory. People have many times asked how it seems that we are so blessed. We know that it is only the goodness of the Lord. We believe that obedience to the Lord can curry his favor and His special grace and love will be bestowed upon us.

3. *You will be kept out of the "Great Tribulation".*

This really is a promise to all those who live an overcoming life. Just to think that when the Anti-Christ finally is revealed and comes to do his dirty work upon the earth for some 3 ½ years, we will be kept out of that terrible hour by the grace of our Lord Jesus.

A SPECIAL CHALLENGE TO PHILADELPHIA

"Behold, I come quickly; hold that fast which thou hast, that no man take thy crown!"

Those who are living in Philadelphia grace and glory have received that precious crown of His anointing. They are living in the promises of the Word of God and know that Psalm One has been given to them and to all who will believe it and walk in it.

"Blessed is the man that walketh not in the counsel of the ungodly, nor standeth in the way of sinners, nor sitteth in the seat of the scornful. But his delight is in the law of the Lord; and in his law doth he meditate day and night. And he shall be like a tree planted by the rivers of water, that bringeth forth his fruit in his season; his leaf also shall not wither; and <u>whatsoever he doeth shall prosper!</u>"

Philadelphians, hang on to your crown of blessing! Don't let anyone take it from you. It is yours to possess and have for eternity. Cherish your heritage given you by the Lord for your faithfulness.

THE PROMISE TO THE OVERCOMERS

1. *"He that overcometh will I make a pillar in the temple of my God."*

The pillar is that part of the foundation, which holds up the superstructure of the whole building. It is vital to the building. Remember the story of strong man Samson.

God avenged him of his enemies in Judges 16:28-30, *"And Samson called unto the Lord, and said, O Lord God, remember me, I pray thee, and strengthen me, I pray thee, only this once, O God, that I may be at once avenged of the Philistines for my two eyes. And Samson took hold of the two middle <u>pillars upon which the house stood</u> ... And he bowed himself with all his might; and the house fell upon the lords, and upon all the people that were within. So the dead which he slew at his death were more than they which he slew in his life."*

The Apostle Paul declared in Ephesians 2:20-22, *"Ye are built upon the foundation of the apostles and prophets, Jesus Christ himself being the chief corner stone. In whom all the building fitly framed together groweth unto an holy temple in the Lord; In whom ye also are builded together for an habitation of God through the Spirit."*

As overcomers, we will be a major part of the eternal temple and habitation of the Living God and *"go no more out"*. Secure forever in Christ!

2. *"I will write upon him the name of my God."*

When a woman is married, she takes on the name of her husband. We will be forever married to Him *"who loved us and gave himself for us"*. We cannot be ashamed of His Name now and expect to be overcomers because His name is the name that we shall bear for all eternity. In God's Word, 'name' denotes 'nature'. When we take on the name of the Lord Jesus, we take on His nature.

3. *"And the name of the City of my God."*

This city, the New Jerusalem, will be the eternal habitation of the Bride of Christ. She will go in and out to the nations on the New Earth with the leaves of the Tree of Life for their healing.

"Come hither, I will shew thee the Bride, the Lamb's wife. And he carried me away in the Spirit to a great and high mountain, and shewed me that great city, the Holy Jerusalem, descending out of heaven from God!" (Rev. 21:9,10).

"And the leaves of the tree (of life) were for the healing of the nations (on the new earth)." (Rev. 22:2).

4. *"And I will write upon him my new name."*

The Lord also promised the overcomers in the Church of Pergamos that they would have *"a new name"*. I asked the Lord why they, the overcomers, would get a new name in glory. The only answer I could find is that Jesus said, *"Behold, I make all things new!"* (Rev. 21:5). My name, Glenyce, has always been a difficult one to pronounce and only once in my life did I find someone with a name spelled just like mine. In eternity, I will get used to a new name and it should be easier than the one I have now.

So here we end the teaching of the most wonderful church age of all, that of Philadelphia. I trust that you have enjoyed this study and will strive to be a part of the 'Church of Brotherly Love' in spite of living in the 'Lukewarm' church age.

LAODICEA
The Lukewarm Church

Revelation 3:14-22:

14. *And unto the angel of the church of the Laodiceans write; These things saith the Amen, the faithful and true witness, the beginning of the creation of God.*

15. *I know thy works that thou art neither cold nor hot; I would thou wert cold or hot.*

16. *So then because thou art lukewarm, and neither cold nor hot, I will spue thee out of my mouth.*

17. Because thou sayest, I am rich, and increased with goods, and have need of nothing; and knowest not that thou art wretched, and miserable, and poor, and blind, and naked.

18. I counsel thee to buy of me gold tried in the fire that thou mayest be rich, and white raiment, that thou mayest be clothed, and that the shame of thy nakedness do not appear; and anoint thine eyes with eyesalve that thou mayest see.

19. As many as I love, I rebuke and chasten; be zealous therefore, and repent.

20. Behold, I stand at the door and knock; if any man hear my voice, and open the door, I will come in to him, and sup with him, and he with me.

21. To him that overcometh will I grant to sit with me in my throne, even as I also overcame, and am set down with my Father in his throne.

22. He that hath an ear, let him hear what the Spirit saith unto the churches.

FACTS ABOUT LAODICEA

Laodicea completes the series of the Seven Churches of Asia. It brings us up to present time of the 21ST Century. The city of Laodicea is now gone from history. It was located in that day ten miles from Colossae. In John's day it was a great metropolitan center of commerce and, even then, a very worldly place having the pagan god, Zeus, as their deity. As late as the fourth century an important church council was held in Laodicea, this indicates there was still a church present at that time.

The name Laodicea means *"the rights of the people"*. How aptly it sets forth this age when the Lukewarm Church goes on its own way paying no heed to the Word of God or the prophets of the Lord. If you have been a Christian any number of years, you must see the 'Signs of the times' and the condition of the church in general compared to the many years past. Strangely enough, we know that 'all truth is parallel'. This means that while there is a lukewarm church there is also an 'on-fire church' that is preparing a bride for the coming Bridegroom. While the historical church of Laodicea is long gone, the spirit of Laodicea greatly remains in the earth and in the church today as we shall clearly see.

THE ANGEL/MESSENGER OF LAODICEA

Because it is the end-time, as spoken of so much in the Word of God, there cannot be pinpointed one who was the messenger of this last church age. Instead, God has raised up a 'Five-fold Ministry' that will function in all of the Gifts of the Spirit that He has so clearly defined in His Word.

And he gave some <u>apostles</u>, and some <u>prophets</u>, and some <u>evangelists</u>, and some <u>pastors</u> and (some) <u>teachers</u>. For the perfecting of the saints (church), for the work of the ministry, for the edifying of the Body of Christ. Till we all come in the unity of the faith, and of the knowledge of the Son of God, unto a perfect (mature) man, unto the measure of the stature of the fullness of Christ!

(Eph.4:11-13)

Note: For those who would say that a woman cannot fulfill all of these ministry gifts to the church, please look at this fact. The word 'some' used in this text is taken from the Greek word 'ho', which indicates, both male and female. Hence, this text can be read like this, *"And he gave some (ho) male and female apostles ... etc."*

1. *The Apostle – The thumb of the five-fold ministry.*

Like Paul, who is the great example, the Apostle is the first one on the scene, the pioneer, the planter. It is the

Apostle who establishes the order of things and sets the base for the future of the work of God. It is the Apostle who literally has his/her 'thumb' on the situation as the action of the work unfolds.

Neither my husband or I have ever used this term to describe our ministry, and ourselves and yet, by the very things we have done for more than sixty years, we qualify to be called 'Apostle' for the very works sake.

2. *The Prophet* – The Prophet is the index finger of the five-fingered hand of the ministry. This finger points the way, points to the past and the future with the Rhema Word of God. Like the old war posters of Uncle Sam pointing and saying "I want you!" so the Prophet does the very same thing in the Body of Christ today. Paul was very clear when, in Ephesians 2:20, he let the church know of their foundation.

"And are built upon the foundation of the <u>APOSTLES</u> and <u>PROPHETS</u>, Jesus Christ himself being the chief corner stone!"

3. *The Evangelist* – The Evangelist is the longest finger of the ministry hand. It stands taller than any of the others just like the Evangelist even today is the one who is the best known. Great evangelists like D.L. Moody, Billy Sunday, Billy Graham, Oral Roberts are all very well known around the world, whereas, little pastors, who stay by the stuff and work in the local field, are hardly ever recognized except by our righteous Lord.

4. *The Pastor* – The Pastor is recognized by the ring finger because he is married to the local church. A true pastoral calling follows the admonition of the Scriptures which declare, *"Feed the flock of God which is among you, taking the oversight thereof, not by constraint, but willing; not for filthy lucre, but of a ready mind."* (1 Pet.5:2).

5. *The Teacher* – The teacher is represented by the little finger. When we want to clean out our ears, we don't go in with the thumb or even one of our other fingers, we use the 'pinky', the little finger. Do it unconsciously and see for yourself. So it is that the teacher feeds us the Word into the *"hearing of the ear"*. The Bible talks about the last days when many will listen to false teachers in this luke-warm age.

    "For the time will come (Laodicea) when they will not endure sound doctrine; but heap to themselves teachers, having itching EARS; And they shall turn away their ears from the truth, and shall be turned into fables." (2 Tim. 4:3,4).

CHRIST'S CONDEMNATION OF LAODICEA

Because of the Lukewarm Age, Christ could not really commend the Laodiceans for any good works. There were, of course, overcomers in the church even as there is in this our day. To them the Lord gives His promise as He did to all other overcomers in every church age.

1. *"I know thy works"* – Jesus saw their works that they were not done because of their love for Christ, but were done out of a religious spirit of 'good works' trying to earn God's favor. This can never work because the Lord looks on the heart.

2. *"Thou art neither cold nor hot"* – Then, of all things, the Lord goes on to say, *"I would thou wert cold or hot!"* This phrase is a real stumbler. It is understandable why the Lord wants His Church to be on fire and 'hot' for Him, but why 'cold'? This is hard to understand until we see what He is really saying. The Lord is telling His people that He wants us to be on the mountaintop of victory and on fire – HOT - for Him.

    When we are walking with Him in victory, the Holy Spirit fills our hearts with that warm anointing and truly all is well. But there are also those seasons when we carry burdens for our loved ones or for special needs and in those times we are called to fast and pray for things. These times are not those shouting times, but the – COLD – sacrificial times of reaching out to God. In those times of sacrifice, we don't feel like shouting and dancing, but rather weeping before the Lord. This is the meaning here by being 'hot' or 'cold'.

We took note in our worldwide travels that in almost every nation in the bathrooms, the hot faucet is denoted by the color red and the cold one by the color blue so that there is a definite distinction. What do you get when you mix those two colors? You get purple or scarlet which is a type of Babylon which we shall see when we get to Revelation 17.

3. *"Thou art wretched, and miserable, and poor, and blind, and naked!"*

Wow! What words from the mouth of the Lord. What a state to be in, thinking they were *"rich, increased with goods, having need of nothing"* only to find out from Jesus that they were just the opposite in His eyes. Oh, the lesson we must learn from this age that we cannot allow ourselves to sit back and take our ease thinking everything is just fine when perhaps it is not.

Let us examine our hearts and our motives to see if they match up to what the Lord requires of us. We are 'old-timers' in the move of the Holy Spirit and things we see in the church today are so different from what they were in the early days. We are not here to criticize, but only to pray that the overcomers will keep on keeping on for Jesus 'til He comes in the clouds of glory.

A SPECIAL WORD TO LAODICEA

"I counsel thee to buy of me gold tried in the fire that thou mayest be rich; and white raiment, that thou mayest be clothed, and that the shame of thy nakedness do not appear; and anoint thine eyes with eyesalve that thou mayest see."

1. *"Gold tried in the fire!"* – Peter tells us that the trial of our faith is even more precious than that of gold. Gold in today's market is the most precious commodity and it holds its value unlike normal money such as dollars or euros. The 'gold' of a Christ-like character is something to be desired. As people see Christ in us, they will know that they have been with Jesus.

2. *"White raiment"* – We already shared about the three kinds of garments for the saints in eternity. 'White raiment' speaks of the garment of rulership that those who rule around His throne will wear. He wants us to start down here by ruling our flesh and our situations and take our authority over the enemy to lead a victorious life.

3. *"Anoint thine eyes with eyesalve"* – What wondrous things we see when the precious Holy Spirit anoints our spiritual eyes with His ointment. The Spirit reveals to us where we really are that we may seek the Lord to be in the place of His perfect will. An old hymn of the church said this: "Open my eyes that I may see; Glimpses of truth Thou hast for me ..." He wants to show us His Glorious Truth!

4. *"Be zealous and repent!"* – We are challenged of the Lord to be zealous and on fire for Him and repent of our lethargy and lack of zeal for His Kingdom.

CHRIST IS KNOCKING AT THE DOOR!

"Behold, I stand at the door and knock; if any man hear my voice, and open the door, I will come in to him, and will sup with him, and he with me!"

This verse of Scripture does not just refer to Christ's knocking at the door of the sinful heart as we so many times hear preached. It refers in context to the church of Jesus Christ in this end-time. We are caught up so many times with our programs and our forms of religion that we don't have room for Jesus in it all.

Many years ago when my mother-in-law was still living, we were looking at a lovely manger scene in a department store window. While admiring its beauty and thanking God that Christ was still in Christmas, two well-dressed ladies stood by and made this comment, "Isn't it something that they even have to bring religion into Christmas."

Let it never be said that we have brought religion into our worship. It is so easy to be religious and yet lost. Jesus is knocking at the door of the End-time Church and saying, "Let Me be the center of it all; not your forms, not your rituals, not even your three fast songs and three slow ones; just Me and Me alone!"

THE PROMISE TO THE OVERCOMERS

"To him that overcometh, will I grant to sit with me in my throne, even as I also overcame, and am set down with my Father in his throne!"

This is one of my favorite promises to the overcomers. So many times when we have preached the overcoming message, my husband has illustrated it so perfectly. He will call a young couple out of the audience. Then sitting down on a chair in front of the crowd, he asks the young man to sit on his lap. Bob represents the Father *"sitting on His throne"*. The young man types the Son, who overcame, *"sitting in the throne with His Father"*. Then the young man's wife, his bride, sits down on his lap representing the overcoming Bride of Christ *"sitting on His throne with Him even as He is set down with the Father in His throne"*.

What a picture of how it will be in the heavenlies when the Bride of Christ , the true Queen of Heaven, sits in the throne with Christ even as He sits in the throne with His Father, one Eternal Throne seating the Godhead and the Bride. It may look impossible in the natural, but we already know that *"with God all things are possible!"*

What a day that will be when our Jesus we shall see; When we look upon His face, the one who saved us by His grace. When He takes us by the hand and leads us through that promised land; What a day, glorious day that will be.

CHAPTER 4

AFTER THIS

The Apostle John was commanded to write concerning three classes of things:

1. Things past – *"The things which thou hast seen"* which is the Patmos vision on the island where John was exiled to die.

2. Things present – meaning the things that were existing at that time including the Seven Churches of Asia.

3. Things to come – those things that were to happen after the Church Age was finished.

John's spirit, not his body, was carried into heaven by the Holy Ghost and he was shown the future and the ages to come. He saw the Lord on His throne, the angelic hosts, the four living creatures, the elders around the throne and many more things.

"I Jesus have sent mine angel to testify unto you these things in the churches. I am the root and the offspring of David, and the bright and morning star. And the Spirit and the bride say, Come. And let him that heareth say, Come. And let him that is athirst come. And whosoever will, let him take the water of life freely."

(Rev.22:16,17)

John's visit to heaven was told us by his experience of being there. He is showing us these things that we might understand these end times and what our experience will be at the coming of the Lord. After all of John's 'revelation' experiences, God miraculously delivered him from the Isle of Patmos and brought him to Ephesus where he lived out the remainder of his earthly life. It was there he cared for the Virgin Mary until her death as the Lord had commanded him whilst He was on the cross. History tells us that John the Beloved went to be with the Lord at about 94 years of age.

The Bible says, *"... to be absent from the body, and to be present with the Lord!"* (2 Cor. 5:8).

On Patmos, John's spirit left his body to be in the heavenlies, but his body was still alive perhaps in a trance. Now, at the end of his life, his spirit and soul leave his now dead body and go to be with the Lord until the resurrection day.

Here in Revelation 4, we see a perfect picture of *"the catching away"* of the overcomers in Jesus Christ. We have often called it 'THE RAPTURE' though this exact term is not used in the Bible. The word 'rapture' is not a doctrine. It is simply a word used to describe what will take place at the coming of the Lord Jesus. Webster's Dictionary defines 'rapture' thus: "Being carried away with great joy."

Second Thessalonians 4:13-18 describes what will happen when the Lord Jesus comes for His Overcoming Church in the clouds of glory:

"But I would not have you to be ignorant, brethren, concerning them which are asleep, that ye sorrow not, even as others which have no hope. For this we say unto you by the word of the Lord, that we which are alive and remain unto the coming of the Lord shall not prevent (precede) them which are asleep. For the Lord himself shall descend from heaven with a shout, with the voice of the archangel, and with the trump of God; and the dead in Christ shall rise first; Then we which are alive and remain shall be <u>caught up</u> together with

them in the clouds to meet the Lord in the air; and so shall we ever be with the Lord!"

Just as John was 'raptured' or caught away to heaven in the Spirit of the Lord, we will be caught away at the coming of the Lord following those who died in the Lord including John the Beloved who will be caught up together with us to be with the Lord for all eternity.

There are those who say that this so-called 'rapture' was only brought into the church in the 1800's through a vision given to a young girl in the Brethren Church in England and further propounded by John Darby, author of the Darby Version of the Bible and then by C.I. Schofield, author of the Schofield Reference Bible. It is said that before this time, the theory was not taught. I say that neither was the Baptism of the Holy Spirit taught until the Pentecostal outpouring, or even Justification by Faith until Luther began to expound it. We have learned that God's revealed truth comes in layers and is progressive. All truth is not revealed at one time or we could never take it. Isaiah 28:9,10:

"Whom shall he teach knowledge? And whom shall he make understand doctrine? Them that are weaned from the milk, and drawn from the breasts. For precept must be upon precept, precept upon precept; line upon line, line upon line; here a little, and there a little."

Here are some Bible examples of the 'catching away':

1. Enoch – *"And Enoch walked with God and was not for God took him."* (Gen.5:24).

2. Elijah – *"Elijah went up by a whirlwind into heaven."* (2 Kings 2:11).

3. Jesus Christ – *"While they beheld, he was taken up; and a cloud received him out of their sight."* (Acts 1:9).

4. Old Testament Overcomers – *"And the graves were opened (in Jerusalem); and many bodies of the saints which slept arose; and came out of the graves after his resurrection."* (Matt. 27:52,53).

5. Apostle Paul – *"...such an one (himself) was caught up to the third heaven ... how that he was caught up into paradise."* (2 Cor. 12:2,4).

6. John the Revelator – *"Behold, a door was opened in heaven ... and the voice said, Come up hither!"* (Rev. 4:1).

7. New Testament Overcomers – *"Then we which are alive and remain shall be caught up together with them in the clouds to meet the Lord in the air."* (1 Thess. 4:17).

8. The Two Witnesses – *"And they heard a great voice from heaven saying unto them, Come up hither. And they ascended up to heaven in a cloud."* (Rev. 11:12).

Verse 1:

AFTER THIS I looked, and, behold, a door was opened in heaven; and the first voice which I heard was as it were of a trumpet talking with me; which said, Come up hither, and I will shew thee things which must be hereafter.

"After this" refers to just after the Church Age is finished and the things that will happen following the end of this age. Since Christ's ascension and the coming of the Holy Spirit on the Day of Pentecost, we have been in what is known as the 'Church Age'. It is sometimes referred to as the Age of Grace or the Age of the Holy Spirit. All of these terms are interrelated and interchangeable. We are now in the Third Millennium since all of this began, so we know that the coming of the Lord cannot be too far away.

"After two days (2,000 years) will he revive us; in the third day (now) he will raise us up, and we shall live in his sight. Then shall we

know if we follow on to know the Lord; his going forth is prepared as the morning, and he shall come unto us as the rain, as the latter and former rain unto the earth." (Hosea 6:2,3).

The Apostle Peter declared in Second Peter 3:8, *"That one day is with the Lord as a thousand years, and a thousand years as one day."* It is quite clear from the Word of God that we are living in the *morning of the third day.* The Church Age will soon be ending and the New Day of the Lord will be ushered in upon this earth.

ONE SAT ON THE THRONE

Verses 2,3:

2. *And immediately I was in the Spirit; and, behold, a throne was set in heaven, and ONE sat on the throne.*

3. *And he that sat was to look upon like a jasper and a sardine stone; and there was a rainbow round about the throne in sight like unto an emerald.*

"Immediately" - Paul said it like this in First Corinthians 15:52, *"In a moment in the twinkling of an eye!"* It is going to happen just that fast--no time to get ready or change our ways then. This is why our Lord Jesus admonished us with these words, *"Therefore be ye also ready; for in such an hour as ye think not the Son of Man cometh!"* (Matt. 24:44).

Now, we see from this text that a singular throne was set in heaven and *"one sat on the throne".* I have often pondered this verse wondering how a Triune God could be just one and sit on one throne. We were on one of our mission trips to Jamaica and on the wall of our room there was a calendar from a local funeral home. On the calendar was a painting of heaven with three distinct thrones. On the center one sat a very old man with white hair and a long beard – God the Father. On the right hand side sat a handsome younger man with long golden hair – God the Son. On the other throne was a cloud-like appearance, kind of just a glob – God the Holy Spirit. Is it really going to be like that in the Eternal Heavens? A right understanding of the Triune Godhead would make us to know that while He is Three, He is also One. John 4:24 tells us *"God is a Spirit!"* Of course, we know that the Holy Spirit is a "Spirit", so whose 'body' sitting upon the throne here in this verse?

"There are three that bear record in heaven, the Father, the Word (Son), and the Holy Ghost; and these three are ONE!" (1 John 5:7).

"For in him (Jesus) dwelleth all the fullness of the Godhead <u>bodily</u>; And ye are complete in him, which is the head of all principality and power." (Col. 2:9,10).

Verse 3 in this text tells of this One and describes Him quite clearly using the Old Testament teaching of the stones of the twelve tribes. There were twelve stones in the breastplate worn by the High Priest of Israel. They were set in rows and represented the twelve tribes of Israel. The first stone was that of the firstborn son, Reuben. His stone was the *"sardine stone"*. This stone was called the *"blood stone"* as it had streaks of red like blood running through it. Reuben's name means "Behold a son!" Who was the Son of the Living God? Who was streaked with blood for our redemption? Who was *"the firstborn among many brethren"* as it tells us in Romans 8:29?

Then we see the *"jasper stone"*. This stone belonged to the youngest and last son, Benjamin. His name means "Son of my right hand!" The *"jasper stone"* was *"clear as crystal"* according to Revelation 21:11. The Word is clear when it tells us that Jesus Christ is *"Alpha and Omega, the first and the last!"* according to Revelation 1:11. We also know that He is *"the beginning and the ending"*, so who else could it be that sits upon the throne except He who is *"altogether lovely"* (Song of Songs 5:16).

It goes on to tell us *"there was a rainbow round about the throne in sight like unto an <u>emerald</u>."* This rainbow did not go like an arc in the sky as we would imagine it to be. This rainbow went around the throne like a circle. There was a reason for this as well. It was like unto *"an emerald"*. The emerald was the stone of Judah. We know that Judah means "praise". Around the throne of our God like a rainbow is "praise" forever and ever. The Judah praises of God's redeemed! Judah was the first to go into battle with the praises of the Lord. Praise makes a way when all else seems to fail. And remember that our Jesus is *"the Lion of the tribe of Judah!"* (Rev. 5:5).

Send Judah first and the battle will be won. Send Judah first and the foe is overcome.

Giving praise to the Father and glory to the Son. Send Judah first!

The Judah praises will be round about the throne as a shining emerald forever and ever!

THE TWENTY-FOUR ELDERS

Verses 4,5:

4. *And round about the throne were four and twenty seats; and upon the seats I saw four and twenty elders sitting, clothed in white raiment; and they had on their heads crowns of gold.*

5. *And out of the throne proceeded lightnings and thunderings and voices; and there were seven lamps of fire burning before the throne, which are the seven Spirits of God.*

Here we see twenty-four special seats round about the throne of God. Sitting on these seats were twenty-four ruling elders, the governors of heaven as it were. These were likely representative of the twelve tribes of Israel and of the twelve Apostles of the Lamb. Note that they wore *"white raiment"* which was one of the three types of garments worn in eternity. The great multitude of redeemed will wear *"white robes"* as they worship and serve God day and night. The Bride of Christ will wear *"white linen"* depicting the special garments given to those who have become one with Christ. This raiment given to these twenty-four elders spoke of ruling and authority. They also had on their heads *"crowns of gold"* denoting kingly rulers and authority as well.

Out of the throne came the awesomeness of our God demonstrated by *"lightnings and thunderings and voices"* as He let His Glory be known even unto those before and around the throne. The seven lamps of fire burning before the throne, we already discussed in chapter 1. They represented the Seven Spirits of God, which were from God's Throne and later *"sent forth into all the earth"* (Rev. 5:6). Many times in Scripture, fire is used to describe God and His Spirit, as truly *"God is a consuming fire!"* (Heb.12:29).

It is interesting to see how the nine Gifts of the Holy Spirit, as enumerated in First Corinthians 12:8-10, dovetail with these Seven Spirits of God. In reality it is the "Seven-fold Spirit of God" as we know that there is only one Holy Spirit or Holy Ghost which are two terms denoting that *"one and the selfsame Spirit"*.

THE FOUR LIVING CREATURES

Verses 6-8:

6. *And before the throne there was a sea of glass like unto crystal; and in the midst of the throne, and round about the throne, were four beasts (living creatures) full of eyes before and behind.*

7. *And the first beast was like a lion, and the second beast like a calf, and the third beast had a face as a man, and the fourth beast was like a flying eagle.*

8. And the four beasts had each of them six wings about him; and they were full of eyes within; and they rest not day and night, saying, Holy, holy, holy, Lord God Almighty, which was, and is, and is to come!

We see here that before God's throne there was *"a sea of glass"*. Several hymns and songs have been written about that glassy sea. We have watched the setting sun on the South China Sea in Northern Luzon in the Philippines where we have spent so much of our missionary time over the past thirty-five or more years. It has always been the most beautiful scene and seemed to bring us close to God and heaven especially when the sea was as calm as glass. How much more will it be when we shall see and even walk on that heavenly *"sea of glass"* before the throne of God? It also says that it was *"like unto crystal"*.

Three times in the Book of Revelation, we see this word *"crystal"* mentioned.

1. THE SEA – *"a sea of glass like unto <u>crystal</u>"* (4:6).

2. THE STONE – *"her light (The Holy City) was like unto a stone most precious, even like a jasper stone, clear as <u>crystal</u>."* (21:11).

3. THE RIVER – *"And he shewed me a pure river of water of life, clear as <u>crystal</u>, proceeding out of the throne of God and of the Lamb."* (22:1).

Now, the 'Four Living Creatures', the King James Version calls them *"beasts"*, were not really beasts as we think of such. The Greek word used here is only used of these creatures and is *"zoon"*[1] taken from the root *"zao"*[2] meaning *"a living thing or creature"*. We often think of the *"beast"* of the Apocalypse as being the anti-Christ as he is called that several times which we shall study later. The Greek word *"beast"* there is the word

---

[1] (Strong's #2226)
[2] (#2198)

"therion"[3] and means "a very dangerous or venomous wild beast".

As we look further at these 'Four Living Creatures', we see that the Prophet Ezekiel saw them in a vision as well as the Apostle John. This is how he describes them, *"Also out of the midst thereof came the likeness of four <u>living creatures</u>. And this was their appearance ... As for the likeness of their faces, they four had the face of a <u>man</u>, and the face of a <u>lion</u> on the right side; and they four had the face of an <u>ox</u> on the left side; they four also had the face of an <u>eagle</u>."*

Here we have it in both the Old and the New Testaments – 'The Four Living Creatures'. One of the greatest preachers of the Twentieth Century was none other than Aimee Semple McPherson, founder of the Foursquare Gospel Churches and the great Angelus Temple at Echo Park in Los Angeles, California. The doors of this amazing building were officially opened on January 1, 1923 to the swelling of the great organ. Her favorite verse from God's Word was emblazoned upon the front wall and is there to this day. It is Hebrews 13:8, "JESUS CHRIST THE SAME, YESTERDAY, AND TODAY, AND FOREVER!"

In that day, Angelus Temple drew crowds of 25,000 people each week and it was for many years America's Mega Church. Through the years, thousands were fed both the Word of God and natural food in what was known as the "bread lines". Sister Aimee, as she was affectionately called, had a vision as she was studying Ezekiel and saw these creatures as being a type of the Lord Jesus Christ.

1. "THE MAN" – The man Christ Jesus who, coming to this earth as a man, *"became sin for us who knew no sin"* and, thus, this depicts SALVATION.

---

[3] (#2342)

2. "THE LION" – This depicts the Lord Jesus as *"the Lion of the tribe of Judah"* and the mighty BAPTISM IN THE HOLY SPIRIT.

3. "THE OX (CALF)" – She saw Jesus as the great burden-bearer who *"himself carried our infirmities and bore our sicknesses"* thus He brought us DIVINE HEALING.

4. "THE EAGLE" – The mighty eagle soaring into the heavenlies brought Sister Aimee the vision of the Second Coming of Christ. This completed the fourth plank of her 'Foursquare Church'. Jesus Christ THE SOON-COMING KING.

Here was our Lord Jesus depicted in The Four Living Creatures as Savior, Healer, Baptizer in the Holy Spirit and Soon-Coming King. This teaching has been the cornerstone of Pentecostal/Charismatic Churches down through the 20TH Century and now into the 21ST Century. What began as a small 'mustard seed' now covers the whole earth.

God's promise in His Word was this, *"But as truly as I live, all the earth shall be filled with the glory of the Lord!"* (Numb. 14:21). *"For the earth shall be filled with the knowledge of the glory of the Lord, as the waters cover the sea!"* (Hab. 2:14).

FALLING OUT IN THE SPIRIT

Verses 9-11:

9. *And when those beasts give glory and honour and thanks to him that sat on the throne, who liveth forever and ever.*

10. *The four and twenty elders fall down before him that sat on the throne, and worship him that liveth forever and ever, and cast their crowns before the throne, saying*

11. *Thou art worthy, O Lord, to receive glory and honour and power; for thou hast created all things, and for thy pleasure they are and were created.*

The manifestation in Charismatic and Pentecostal Churches of "falling out in the Spirit" or "resting in the Lord", as some have come to call it, or as the phrase was coined during the days of the Toronto Outpouring, "doing carpet time" is nothing new in these recent times. History records this type of thing as far back as there was any kind of move of the Holy Ghost. Here in Revelation is a similar type of thing happening which just may have been a Scriptural forerunner of such a thing.

Four times the Twenty-four Elders and the Four Living Creatures are seen to *"fall down"* in God's presence.

1. *"The four and twenty elders fall down before him that sat on the throne!"* (Revelation 4:10).

2. *"The four beasts (living creatures) and four and twenty elders fell down before the Lamb!"* (5:8).

3. *"And the four and twenty elders fell down and worshipped him that liveth forever and ever!"* (5:14).

4. *"And all the angels stood round about the throne, and the elders and the four beasts (living creatures) fell before the throne on their faces, and worshipped God."* (7:11).

These words *"fall"* and *"fell"* come from the Greek word "pipto"[4] meaning simply "to fall down or fall out" which is what happened here. In the early days of our ministry, we had heard about a healing evangelist named Lorne Fox who went around in tent meetings and had this manifestation happen to hundreds in his meetings. We drove one night to visit the big tent, but both my husband and I were not at all convinced about this 'falling out' stuff so we were pretty well determined that it would not happen to us.

---

[4] (Strong's #4098)

Rev. Fox had all the crowd line up around the tent walls facing the center. Following along with the preacher as he went around that circle were 'catchers' who stood behind the people as the man of God passed by. This was a first for us so we looked on with amazement. Everyone he touched 'fell out' and some laid there as if they were dead. My husband braced himself for what was coming, but to no avail. Before the evangelist ever got to him, he just looked at Bob, pointed his finger, and down went the skeptic.

This was only the beginning of so many times when neither one of us could stand under the mighty power of God. In the sixty nations where we have ministered God's Word and prayed for thousands, it is not at all uncommon for many that we touch, or some that we do not touch at all, to fall or go down under the power of the Lord. Falling does not make you any more or any less spiritual than one who does not have this experience. It is simply a precious time with Jesus, as you lay before Him in the glory oblivious of all that is around you. More times than not, those who arise from the floor following this experience speak of visions or a fresh touch of God. Most all declare that they were touched by God and healed or at least felt so much better than before. To God be the glory for all that He does to us mortal humans. Hallelujah!

CHAPTER 5

THE LION AND THE LAMB

In this chapter of the Apocalypse we see the magnificent portrayal of our Lord Jesus as the mighty "LION OF THE TRIBE OF JUDAH" who was able *"to loose the seven seals"* of the book. He then takes on the humble nature of "THE SLAIN LAMB OF GOD" to share with us His glorious redemption. Let's take a look at this beautiful picture that John presents to the readers of Revelation.

Verses 1-5:

1. *And I saw in the right hand of him that sat on the throne a book written within and on the backside, sealed with seven seals.*

2. *And I saw a strong angel proclaiming with a loud voice, Who is worthy to open the book, and to loose the seals thereof?*

3. *And no man in heaven, nor in earth, neither under the earth, was able to open the book, neither to look thereon.*

4. *And I wept much, because no man was found worthy to open and to read the book, neither to look thereon.*

5. *And one of the elders saith unto me, Weep not: behold, the <u>Lion of the tribe of Judah</u> hath prevailed to open the book, and to loose the seven seals thereof.*

Now, while *"the Lion of the tribe of Judah"* actually has the power to loose the seven seals, it is *"the Lamb"* who actually opens the seals according to Revelation 6:1, *"And I saw when the Lamb opened one of the seals!"*

The *Lion* and the *Lamb* are one and the selfsame person, the *Son of the Living God,* who is able to do all things according the power of His own will. This whole study of Revelation is for one purpose - to bring us all closer to the Lord Jesus Christ, our Heavenly Bridegroom and Soon-coming King.

Verse 6:

And I beheld, and, lo, in the midst of the throne and of the four beasts (living creatures), and in the midst of the elders, stood a Lamb as it had (just) been slain, having seven horns and seven eyes, which are the seven Spirits of God sent forth into all the earth.

THE PRECIOUS LAMB OF GOD

It is wonderful to note in the above text that this *"Lamb of God"* appears as one who had *'just been slain'.* In other words His blood was still fresh and life-giving. When John the Baptist saw Jesus coming across the Judean hillside, he cried out to the multitude, *"Behold, the Lamb of God which taketh away the sin of the world!"* (John 1:29). Now, we see this Lamb in Revelation already slain for the sins of the world as John the Baptist said.

This study in Revelation is not to present other subjects such as the blood of Christ and its power to redeem and wash clean. Many books have been written about it to the glory of God. Our cry in these last days is that the church will never lose sight of the power of the precious blood. All too many of our new songs and choruses contain nothing about the blood of Christ. Seldom are sermons preached about the subject.

While I was ministering some time ago at White Horse Christian Center in West Lafayette, Indiana, I made this statement concerning the blood. Pastor Jeff Johns, being keen in the Spirit, picked up on it and began a wonderful series on the blood. Men and women of God, who read this book, please always keep the blood of Christ prominent in your preaching.

What can wash away my sin?

> Nothing but the blood of Jesus.
> What can make me whole again?
> Nothing but the blood of Jesus!
> O, precious is the flow
> That makes me white as snow;
> No other fount I know;
> Nothing but the blood of Jesus!

Many years ago, my husband had a one-time experience that he has never forgotten. He was praying on his knees on the platform of our church before the service. He was all alone in the sanctuary when, suddenly, he felt an awesome unseen presence. As he looked down at his open Bible, there was a large drop of fresh blood. He put his finger on it and it was still wet. Thinking that perhaps he had scratched his head, he felt of it but there was no blood there. It then dawned upon him that God had simply made the unseen blood to be seen for just that moment so we could never forget to preach it as the only way of salvation. No issue was ever made of it, but he has that Bible and the spot of blood marking it to this day.

"And almost all things are by the law purged with blood; and without the shedding of blood there is no remission (of sin)!" (Heb. 9:22). The precious Lamb of God not only had fresh blood, but He had *"seven horns and seven eyes which are the seven Spirits of God"* We have already shared with you those Seven Spirits of God, but what about the *"seven horns and seven eyes"*. The *'seven horns'* speak of the power of the Lamb and we know He is *'omnipotent'*.

The *'seven eyes'* let us know that our Lord is also *'omniscient'*, that is the All-knowing God who sees everything before it ever happens. Then to round out His three attributes, we also know that He is *'omnipresent'*. No matter where we go, He is there. The Psalmist David said it so beautifully in Psalm 139, *"Whither shall I go from thy Spirit; or whither shall I flee from thy presence? If I ascend up into heaven, thou art there; if I make my bed in hell, behold, thou art there. If I take the wings of the morning, and dwell in the uttermost parts of the sea; Even there shall thy hand lead me, and thy right hand shall hold me!"*

Omniscient - Omnipotent - Omnipresent that's our wonderful God revealed to us as Father, Son and Holy Spirit, all possessing every one of the attributes of the other in perfect unity and harmony. Like the majestic hymn of the church that we have sung so many times declares, "God in three persons, Blessed Trinity!"

SEVEN – A SPECIAL NUMBER

Seven is a number that appears so many times in the Book of Revelation. In our study, we have found seventeen different categories of 'seven':

1. Churches	(1:4,11,20)
2. Spirits	(1:4; 3:1; 4:5; 5:6)
3. Candlesticks	(1:12,20; 2:1)
4. Stars	(1:16,20; 2:1; 3:1)
5. Lamps of fire	(4:5)
6. Seals	(5:1,5)
7. Horns	(5:6)
8. Eyes	(5:6)
9. Angels	(8:2,6; 15:1,6,7,8; 16:1; 17:1; 21:9)
10. Trumpets	(8:2,6)
11. Thunders	(10:3,4)
12. Heads	(12:3; 13:1; 17:3,7,9)
13. Crowns	(12:3)
14. Plagues	(15:1,6,8; 21:9)
15. Golden vials	(15:7; 17:1; 21:9)
16. Mountains	(17:9)
17. Kings	(17:10)

Does it seem strange, that with all of the emphasis on the number 'seven' in the Book of Revelation, not once is the term

'Seven Years of Great Tribulation' ever mentioned? We have always taught that the number seven represents completeness or fullness. From the seven-branch lamp stand of the Old Testament, also found in Revelation, to the multitude of sevens in our current study, there is no question that it is a favorite number in the Scriptures. Yet, no seven years tribulation is ever mentioned. Think about it!

THE AWESOME WORSHIP OF THE LORD

Verses 7-14:

7. *And he came and took the book out of the right hand of him that sat upon the throne.*

8. *And when he had taken the book, the four beasts (living creatures) and four and twenty elders fell down before the Lamb, having every one of them harps, and golden vials full of odours, which are the prayers of saints.*

9. *And they sung a new song saying, Thou art worthy to take the book, and to open the seals thereof; for thou wast slain, and hast redeemed us to God by thy blood out of every kindred, and tongue, and people, and nation;*

10. *And hast made us unto our God kings and priests; and we shall reign on the earth.*

11. *And I beheld, and I heard the voice of many angels round about the throne and the beasts and the elders; and the number of them was ten thousand times ten thousand, and thousands of thousands;*

12. *Saying with a loud voice, Worthy is the Lamb that was slain to receive power, and riches, and wisdom, and strength, and honour, and glory, and blessing.*

13. *And every creature which is in heaven, and on the earth, and under the earth, and such as are in the sea, and all that are in them, heard I saying, Blessing, and honour, and glory, and power, be unto*

him that sitteth upon the throne, and unto the Lamb forever and ever.

14. *And the four beasts (living creatures) said, Amen! And the four and twenty elders <u>fell down</u> and worshipped him that liveth forever and ever.*

When George Frederick Handel wrote his famous and wonderful oratorio 'The Messiah', all of this fabulous praise from the Book of Revelation was poured out in this magnificent music. To this very day whenever the finale of this piece, 'The Hallelujah Chorus', is sung, the audience in one accord rises to the occasion. Even though many are not even aware of the greatness of our God, it is as if they are unconsciously being drawn to the Lord.

Each year at the Christmas Season, the Epcot Center at Disney World here in Florida puts on a marvelous concert with a 450-voice choir in lovely costumes along with a full orchestra. Choice Hollywood actors read the Christmas Story from the King James Version of the Holy Bible. All of the music is traditional with no Jingle Bells or Santa Claus. The grand finale is the "Hallelujah Chorus" and the hundreds of guests always stand. We have gone several times and usually there is not a dry eye around us. Many times, we will see people lift their hands in worship to the Lord – at Disney mind you!

The day is soon coming of which Paul spoke when he said in Philippians 2:9-10, *"Wherefore God also hath highly exalted him, and given him a name which is above every name; That at the name of Jesus every knee should bow, of things in heaven, and things in earth, and things under the earth; And that every tongue should confess that Jesus Christ is Lord, to the glory of God the Father!"*

A MULTITUDE TOO GREAT TO NUMBER

Looking ahead to Revelation 7, we see this *"great multitude which no man could number"* while here in our text it gives numbers which can hardly be numbered as well. I tried putting these numbers into my calculator, but it was beyond the capacity of the machine to do it. The world's population is reaching seven billion people. The redeemed of all ages are so great a number that it cannot be numbered.

We must stop listening to the world's news media, which lies to us constantly about everything including the fact that Christianity is obsolete in today's world. The latest polls, from a Christian viewpoint, let us know that there will soon be one billion Pentecostal/Charismatic Christians in the world today. This includes Spirit-filled Catholics. One billion—that's quite a number considering that the Pentecostal Movement is just over a hundred years old. This figure does not include all people professing Christianity as their faith, which adds another billion or more to the number.

The redeemed are chosen from every phase and walk of life from across the entire world. *"The earth is the Lord's, and the fullness thereof; the world, and they that dwell therein!"* (Ps.24:1).

God's chosen and redeemed are taken from every:

1. *"Kindred"* – this refers to families and kinfolk.

   "And I will take you one of a city, and <u>two of a family</u>, and I will bring you to Zion." (Jer. 3:14).

2. *"Tongue"* – all language groups will be there. With the vast variety of dialects in nations, what a blessing it will be to all speak one tongue. Especially in the Philippines, we have found strange dialects even among a particular language group.

3. *"People"* – The Greek word here is "ethnos" from whence we get our word "ethnic groups".

4. *"Nation"* – This was the Great Commission of our Lord Jesus to *"go and teach all nations!"* so that they could be a part of that great company of the redeemed. (See Matt. 28:19).

BIBLICAL HEAVENLY WORSHIP

In this fifth chapter of Revelation, we find some of the greatest worship to the Lord that can be found anywhere in Scripture. It sets a pattern for true Biblical worship in the Body of Christ today. Look with me at four things that comprise this heavenly worship.

1. *Falling before the Lord* (5:8,14).

   Whether it is falling out in the Spirit or the voluntary bowing, kneeling or laying prostrate before the Lord, it is all a part of true worship.

2. *Singing in the Spirit a New Song* (5:9).

   Many years ago a precious couple came to visit our church in Northern Wisconsin. They were from the Zion, Illinois 'Faith Homes'. As the service ended, they asked if they might close in prayer. With our approval, they began to sing in high praise the most beautiful worship unto the Lord. Our church was moved by it and week after week, we found ourselves *'singing in the Spirit'*. If you've never tried it, you will find it is an awesome experience of bringing you close to the Lord.

3. *The Angel Choir Singing* (5:11).

   We will never forget in the days of "The Latter Rain" outpouring how, when we had finished 'singing in the Spirit', it would suddenly be very quiet and then from the heavenlies would come the singing of the 'Angel Choir'. It was truly an unforgettable experience.

4. *Multitudes in Worship* (5:11-13).

This was not man orchestrated worship, this was from the heart of the redeemed, spontaneously given unto the Lord. Oh, that our worship today would become so much that way that we would truly be carried into the realms of God and lost in Him.

It has been said that there is nothing new under the sun. It is the same with our worship unto the Lord. As soon as we think some new form of praise or worship has come along, we will find that some group somewhere have already experienced it. Oh, Lord, give us open hearts to enter into Your glory as You pour it out in these last days upon Your True Church.

CHAPTER 6

THE SEVEN SEALS

Verse 1:

And I saw when the Lamb opened one of the seals, and I heard, as it were the noise of thunder, one of the four beasts (living creatures) saying, Come and see.

THE FOUR HORSEMEN OF THE APOCALYPSE

1. THE WHITE HORSE (Verse 2).

"And I saw, and behold a white horse; and he that sat on him had a bow; and a crown was given unto him; and he went forth conquering, and to conquer."

It has been conjectured by some commentators that this must be the Lord Jesus because the rider is on a 'white horse', but it does not fit the context at all because the other horsemen bring destruction and trouble. No, this is none other than the *'anti-Christ'*, the imitator of the real Christ. He appears as righteous, but lacks true power as we see by the fact that, while he had a bow, he had no arrows to go with it. When he comes, he will deceive many as the Word of God tells us. Let us not be deceived by him. Even in this our day, the enemy comes in a deceptive manner.

Second Corinthians 11:14 tells us,*"And no marvel; for Satan himself is transformed into an angel of light."* The Greek word for "transformed" means 'to be changed into something else'. This is how the enemy functions as he masquerades in something that he really isn't. So it is with this 'white horse' of the Apocalypse.

There is also a spiritual meaning to each of these Four Horsemen along with the literal. The 'white horse' is a picture of 'self-righteousness'. No matter how good we may look, we are never made righteous by anything except the blood of the Lord Jesus. It is very clear from God's Word that *"all our righteousnesses are as filthy rags"* (Isa. 64:6). Let us take heed lest we find ourselves riding the 'white horse of self-righteousness'.

A number of years ago, a leading evangelist whose ministry we loved very much, declared himself to be the greatest preacher currently ministering to the nations and the greatest soul-winner alive. Whilst that 'may have' been the truth, it was not for him to toot his own horn. Not long after, he fell from grace and has never been the same since. It is easy to boast of our works, but let us be careful not to take the glory from the Lord who deserves it all.

2. THE RED HORSE (Verses 3,4).

"And when he had opened the second seal, I heard the second beast (living creature) say, Come and see.

And there went out another horse that was red, and power was given to him that sat thereon to take peace from the earth, and that they should kill one another; and there was given unto him a great sword."

The Second Horseman was riding a 'red horse'. It denotes the time coming when those upon the earth must decide whose side they are on. This passage speaks of the fact that men would *"kill one another"* in the time of the Tribulation. Jesus said in that day, *"And the brother shall deliver up the brother to death, and the father the child; and the children shall rise up against their parents and cause them to be put to death."* (Matt. 10:21).

The color 'red' is used in the Scriptures to denote several things. It is used to describe the great harlot of Revelation. It is used many times in the Old Testament Tabernacle. It describes 'sin' in the prophetic word of Isaiah – *"though your sins be as scarlet, they shall be as white as snow; though they be red like crimson, they shall be as wool."* (1:18). Red is the color of the blood of Jesus, which washes away all sin. But red is also the color of anger.

Spiritually, this was the 'red horse of anger'. When a 'spirit of anger' takes hold of someone, they say and do things, even murder, that they would never do otherwise. We see it happen all the time. Esau, whose name means 'red and hairy' was a perfect example. Amos 1:11 says, *"He did cast off all pity, and his anger did tear perpetually"*.

We must guard ourselves against riding this horse. If we know this truth, let us share it with others so that if anger overtakes them, we can simply say – 'Be careful, you're riding the red horse!' If they understand, they will dismount immediately and be spared. What a lesson to learn that we may take our hurts and frustrations to our Lord Jesus.

3. THE BLACK HORSE (Verses 5,6)

"And when he had opened the third seal, I heard the third beast (living creature) say, Come and see. And I beheld, and lo a black horse; and he that sat on him had a pair of balances in his hand.

And I heard a voice in the midst of the four beasts (living creatures) say, A measure of wheat for a penny, and three measures of barley for a penny, and see thou hurt not the oil and the wine."

This 'black horse' depicts the time of famine that will occur dreadfully during the Great Tribulation. Men will sell their own children for bread. The balances or scales depict how scarce the grain will be as it is weighed out so meticulously. The angel also challenges not to waste or hurt the oil and the wine. Surely, we will not want to be here during that dreadful time upon the earth.

Spiritually speaking, this 'black horse' represents 'carnal reasoning'. What do I mean by that? It is human nature to weigh out things in life, be they good or bad. The same thing applies to the things of God. How easy it is to judge whether a thing is of God or not!

We find ourselves 'weighing out' the 'wheat of the Word'. Most churches today want a twenty-minute sermon on Sunday morning to suffice for the entire week. That is riding the 'black horse of carnal reasoning'

The Word goes on to say, *"see thou hurt not the oil and the wine"*. Oil is a type of the anointing of the Holy Spirit. We must be very careful so we do not grieve the precious Holy Ghost. Wine is a type of the Holy Spirit, but also of the blood of Christ as it is portrayed in the Holy Communion.

We can never do despite to the precious blood of Christ. The spirit of 'carnal reasoning' would tell us to be careful not to go overboard on this 'Spirit stuff'; to weigh out just how much the church can have.

Paul's admonition to us on this subject was, *"Grieve not the Holy Spirit of God, whereby ye are sealed unto the day of redemption!"* (Eph. 4:30).

4. THE PALE HORSE (Verse 8)

"And I looked, and behold a pale horse; and his name that sat on him was Death, and Hell followed with him. And power was given unto them over the fourth part of the earth, to kill with the

sword, and with hunger, and with death, and with the beasts of the earth."

This was a sickly looking pale horse, yellowish green in color representing death by famine, sword and wild beasts during the Tribulation Period which is coming to try them that dwell upon the earth.

Spiritually, it is the 'pale horse of spiritual death'.

If we do not have the Word of God to grow by and we weigh out the Holy Spirit how can we expect to be spiritually alive. Without God's Word and His Spirit to feed upon, we will find ourselves like the 'pale horse', emaciated and sickly and ready to die.

Remember Christ's admonition to the Sardis Church when He said, *"Be watchful, and strengthen the things which remain that are ready to die!"* Many churches and Christians are in this position in the world today and will not be ready for the coming of the Lord. The Lord went on to say to the Sardis Christians, *"If therefore thou shalt not watch, I will come unto thee as a thief, and thou shalt not know what hour I will come unto thee!"* (Rev. 3:3).

Please take a moment and look with me at the Scriptures which proclaim the coming of the Lord as a thief, *"Watch therefore; for ye know not what hour your Lord doth come!"* (Matt.24:42).

"For yourselves know perfectly that the day of the Lord so cometh as a thief in the night!" (1Thess. 5:2). *"But ye, brethren, are not in darkness, that that day should overtake you as a thief!"* (1Thess. 5:4). *"But the day of the Lord will come as a thief in the night!"* (2 Pet.3:10).

"Behold, I come as a thief. Blessed is he that watcheth, and keepeth his garments, lest he walk naked, and they see his shame!" (Rev. 16:15).

THE FIFTH SEAL

Verses 9-11:

9. And when he had opened the fifth seal, I saw under the altar the souls of them that were slain for the word of God, and for the testimony which they held;

10. And they cried with a loud voice, saying, How long, O Lord, holy and true, dost thou not judge and avenge our blood on them that dwell on the earth?

11. And white robes were given unto every one of them; and it was said unto them, that they should rest yet for a little season, until their fellow servants also and their brethren, that should be killed as they were, should be fulfilled.

This group of martyred saints are commonly known as 'the souls under the altar'. Hebrews 13:10 speaks of an altar that the world cannot be a part of and, perhaps, this is that heavenly altar. Nevertheless, we see in this Book of Revelation some further truth concerning the 'heavenly altar'.

"And another angel came and stood at the altar, having a golden censer; and there was given unto him much incense, that he should offer it with the prayers of all saints upon the golden altar which was before the throne of God." (Rev. 8:3).

"And the sixth angel sounded, and I heard a voice from the four horns of the golden altar which is before God." (Rev.9:13).

"And there was given unto me a reed like unto a rod; and the angel stood, saying, Rise, and measure the temple of God, and the altar, and them that worship therein." (Rev. 11:1).

All of the above Scriptures refer to this heavenly *"altar"* under which the martyred souls now dwell. We find that it is before the very throne of God and that it is golden and is a place of worship. These souls *"under the altar"* are in the very presence of the Lord and yet they are there just waiting for a

Divine purpose. Look at this promise of a 'martyr's crown' that awaits these in the day of God's rewards. *"Be thou faithful unto death (as martyrs), and I will give thee a crown of life!"* (Rev. 2:10).

I believe these 'souls under the altar' are those who have been martyred or have given their lives for the cause of the gospel throughout the ages and the Great Tribulation martyrs who never took the 'mark of the beast'. A special crown therefore will be awaiting them in the day of God's rewards to His saints.

There are several kinds of 'crowns' mentioned in the Word of God. It is interesting to look at the different ones.

1. Crown of Glory – *"And when the Chief Shepherd shall appear, ye shall receive a crown of glory that fadeth not away."* (1 Pet. 5:4).

2. Crown of Rejoicing - *"For what is our hope or joy or crown of rejoicing."* (1 Thess. 2:19)

3. Crown of Life – *"Blessed is the man that endureth temptation; for when he is tried, he shall receive the crown of life, which the Lord hath promised to them that love him."* (James 1:12).

4. Crown of Righteousness – *"Henceforth there is laid up for me a crown of righteousness which the Lord, the righteous judge, shall give me in that day; and not to me only, but unto all them also that love his appearing."* (2 Tim. 4:8).

5. Incorruptible Crown – *"Now they do it to receive a corruptible crown; but we an incorruptible crown."* (1Cor. 9:25).

THE SIXTH SEAL

Verses 12-17:

12. And I beheld when he had opened the sixth seal, and, lo, there was a great earthquake; and the sun became black as sackcloth of hair, and the moon became as blood;

13.*And the stars of heaven fell to the earth, even as a fig tree casteth her untimely figs, when she is shaken of a mighty wind.*

14. *And the heaven departed as a scroll when it is rolled together; and every mountain and island were moved out of their places.*

15. *And the kings of the earth, and the great men, and the rich men, and the chief captains, and the mighty men, and every bondman, and every free man, hid themselves in the dens and in the rocks of the mountains;*

16. *And said to the mountains and rocks, Fall on us, and hide us from the face of him that sitteth on the throne, and from the wrath of the Lamb;*

17. *For the great day of his wrath is come; and who shall be able to stand?*

Here we have it – the wrath of Almighty God poured out upon sinful humanity who refused to believe upon Him whilst the door of grace was still open. They saw the gospel on television and mocked it. They passed by the churches that preached Jesus Christ and refused to go in. They had a Bible on every hand, but never read a page of it. What more could God do in His great mercy to reach them than what He had already done. He had sent His Only Begotten Son to die for the sins of humanity. Yet, they would not hear. Now, it was too late, yet they never cried out for mercy from the Lord. They only cried for the mountains and the rocks to fall upon them and kill them.

The Book of Revelation was not written in chronological order so here in chapter six we find the very end of the Great Tribulation portrayed. For many scholars, the Tribulation Period is seven years in length, yet that time length is never once mentioned in the Book of Revelation. I suppose they get the 'Seven-year Tribulation' theory from their interpretation of Daniel's Seventy Weeks found in Daniel 9:24-27. My husband poured himself into the study of Daniel and would not give up until he came up with the truth of what Daniel was talking about. I will share more about that later.

Why do you suppose that this book was not written in chronological order? It would never have reached us in this day for the Roman government would have destroyed it. God had to *"hide these things from the wise and prudent and reveal them unto babes."* These are the words of Jesus found in Matthew 11:25 and Luke 10:25.

Robert Van Kampen, author from Western Michigan, has written much about the end times and the time of tribulation. He calls his theory "The Pre-wrath Rapture". In other words that the 'catching away' of the righteous will take place just prior to the wrath of God being outpoured toward the end of the three and one-half year Tribulation Period. This means of course that the church will go through much of the tribulation under the short reign of the anti-Christ. In this much he is certainly right, that our loving Father in heaven would never pour His wrath out upon His own elect for whom He sent His Son to redeem. No more than a true earthly father would ever pour out his wrath and judgment upon his own children that he loved so much.

Our dear friend, Sister Gwen Shaw, president of the Endtime Handmaidens, had said many times that we will likely go through "Pre-Rapture Tribulation". The church world has always been up in the air about all of these details of the end. The main thing is to keep the main thing the main thing. That 'main thing' is to be ready for His coming at any time. Jesus said, *"Be ye therefore ready, for in such an hour as ye think not, the Son of Man cometh!"* (Matt.24:44; Luke 12:40).

The final 'signs' the Scriptures clearly give as the end of the Dispensation of the Church are given to us here in Chapter 6 at the opening of the 'Sixth Seal'. The identical signs are referred to by the Prophet Joel in 2:30,31 and again by the Apostle Peter on the Day of Pentecost in Acts 2:19,20.

1. The Sun will become dark.
2. The Moon will be turned into blood.
3. The Stars of heaven will fall.
4. A Great Earthquake will occur.

As these things begin to occur at the end of the Tribulation Period, it will be the wrath of Almighty God upon the wickedness of humanity. Thank God that we will not be here. All those who refused to take the 'Mark of the Beast', will be caught up before *that great and notable/terrible day of the Lord* comes.

Chapter Six closes with this admonition, *"For the great day of His wrath is come; and who shall be able to stand?"* (Rev. 6:17).

CHAPTER 7

144,000 SEALED ON EARTH

Chapter 7 of the Apocalypse is a parenthetical chapter prior to the opening of the Seventh Seal, which occurs at the opening of Chapter 8. Chapter 7 is sandwiched in between and really should be placed later, but this is the way Revelation is given to us. Two very specific events are recorded in this chapter, one happening on the earth, the other happening in heaven.

Verses 1-3:

1. *And after these things I saw four angels standing on the four corners of the earth, holding the four winds of the earth, that the wind should not blow on the earth, nor on the sea, nor on any tree.*

2. *And I saw another angel ascending from the east, having the seal of the living God; and he cried with a loud voice to the four angels, to whom it was given to hurt the earth and the sea,*

3. *Saying, Hurt not the earth, neither the sea, nor the trees, till we have sealed the servants of our God in their foreheads.*

The Tribulation is on, but God in His mercy desires to seal a select group of Jews, 12,000 from each tribe, to be sealed in their foreheads so that the anti-Christ and the plagues on the earth cannot touch them. It has been conjectured whether these Jews were Messianic Believers who had accepted the Lord Jesus Christ, but this is questionable. Why? Because at least some of them should have been raptured along with the rest of the overcoming saints. You see, the church is made up of both Jews and Gentiles who have accepted the Lord Jesus Christ as their personal Savior.

It is therefore likely that these chosen Jews are God-loving Israelis who are yet awaiting their Messiah. They are sealed by the Father, awaiting the time when Jesus feet touch the Mount of Olives on His literal return to the earth for the thousand-year Millennial Reign. Look at what the Prophet Zechariah has to say about the Messianic prophecies of that great day.

"And his (Jesus) feet shall stand in <u>that day</u> upon the Mount of Olives, which is before Jerusalem on the east, and the Mount of Olives shall cleave in the midst thereof." (Zech. 14:4).

"And I will pour out upon the House of David, and upon the inhabitants of Jerusalem, the Spirit of grace and of supplications; and they shall look upon me (Jesus) whom they have pierced, and they shall mourn for him, as one mourneth for his only son." (Zech.12:10).

"In <u>that day</u>, there shall be a fountain opened to the House of David and to the inhabitants of Jerusalem for sin and for uncleanness." (Zech.13:1).

There is a fountain filled with blood
Drawn from Emmanuel's veins;
And sinners plunged beneath that flood
Lose all their guilty stains!

Not all Jews, of course, but those who were graciously sealed by God and others of the remnant of Israel, will be saved in that great day of Christ's return to earth.

Verses 4-8:

4. And I heard the number of them which were sealed; and there were sealed an hundred and forty and four thousand of all the tribes of the children of Israel.

5. *Of the tribe of Judah were sealed twelve thousand. Of the tribe of Reuben were sealed twelve thousand. Of the tribe of Gad were sealed twelve thousand.*

6. *Of the tribe of Asher were sealed twelve thousand. Of the tribe of Naphtali were sealed twelve thousand. Of the tribe of Manasseh were sealed twelve thousand.*

7. *Of the tribe of Simeon were sealed twelve thousand. Of the tribe of Levi were sealed twelve thousand. Of the tribe of Issachar were sealed twelve thousand.*

8. *Of the tribe of Zebulon were sealed twelve thousand. Of the tribe of Joseph were sealed twelve thousand. Of the tribe of Benjamin were sealed twelve thousand.*

As we look at the twelve tribes listed, we must take note of some things that are different. First, Levi who was the priestly tribe, was not usually listed with the others, but was really the thirteenth tribe. We know this to be fact because when God was out to choose His High Priest from the Tribe of Levi, there were thirteen rods set before the Tabernacle of the Lord. The rod that budded, as a sign from God, was the rod of Aaron of the Tribe of Levi. We find this story written in Numbers 17.

Next, we see that Ephriam and Manesseh were not included in this list of the sealed tribes, but their father, Joseph, was included to represent both of them.

Finally, Dan was not included at all. This was a mystery to me, until I began to search out the why of this. Dan was not included in this sealing because Dan was the first tribe to be guilty of idol worship in the Promised Land. The first thing that Dan did after they were in Canaan was to break God's statutes by setting up a graven image to which they perversely attributed their success. Along with these false gods, they set up their own substitute for God's guidance.

They rejected the Urim and Thummim of the High Priestly breastplate and substituted a 'teraphim' instead. What in the world is a 'teraphim'? Ezekiel 21:21 says, *"For the king of Babylon stood at the parting of the way, at the head of the two ways, to use divination: he made his arrows bright, he consulted with images (teraphim)."*

This was not a Godly seeking for counsel; this was a Babylonian worldly satanic way to try to find out the future or how to go about a person's next step. In the Book of Judges it tells us clearly of a dreadful time in Israel when every man did what he chose to do without seeking after the Lord.

"In those days there was no king in Israel, but every man did that which was right in his own eyes." (Judg.17:6).

It was during this period that they used divination and false idols to try to discern the will of God. The Tribe of Dan was especially guilty of this sin as we can read in Judges 18 when they inquired, while now in the Promised Land, from false idols named 'teraphim'.

THE URIM AND THUMMIM

Time here will not permit much teaching on these two stones in the breastplate. They were the 'stones of witness' as to the will of God for the Nation of Israel. Inside the breastplate of the high priest of Israel were two precious stones called the 'Urim' and 'Thummim' pronounced in Hebrew 'ooreem' and 'toomeem'.

"And thou shalt put in the breastplate of judgment the Urim and the Thummim; and they shall be upon Aaron's heart when he goeth in before the Lord." (Exod. 28:30).

We are made to understand by the meaning of these stones that when Aaron inquired of the Lord God as to His will on a certain matter, these stones would flash an emphatic "yes" if something was the will of God. When David sought the Lord whether or not to go up to battle against the enemy, I Samuel 30:7,8 says, *"And David said to Abiathar the priest...I pray thee bring me hither the ephod. And Abiathar brought thither the ephod to David. And David inquired of the Lord!"*

What was so important that David needed to have this priestly ephod? In it was the Urim and Thummim of which he inquired of the Lord. The Lord answered David an emphatic "yes" and he went into the battle and won. By the same token, backslidden Saul also thought to inquire of the Lord, but we read these sad words in First Samuel 28:6, *"And when Saul inquired of the Lord, the Lord answered him not, neither by dreams, nor by Urim, nor by prophets."*

By this, we surely know that if we are to hear the voice of God or walk in the will of God, our hearts must be right with Him. Let's look a little more about the Tribe of Dan.

As God always had a remnant from every kindred and every tribe, there will be that remnant out of Dan who will choose for the Lord. We know this to be true, because in the last chapter of Ezekiel there is a list of the new order of the tribes in the Millennium. This is after the event of the sealing recorded here in Revelation and the Tribe of Dan is included. How great is God's eternal mercy!

Further, in our study of Revelation, we will see another group of 144,000 who are also elected of God, but they are not on the earth as this group here. They are in heaven on the Heavenly Mount Zion and represent an entirely different group of people, as we shall later see. Many scholars have grouped them together as one group of this mystical number. A careful study of the two groups will instantly prove different so keep your hearts open to see wondrous truth from God's precious Word.

Our scene now changes in this chapter and we are taken to heaven before the throne of God and see a great multitude like the innumerable group we saw in Chapter 5.

Verses 9-12:

9. *After this I beheld, and, lo, <u>a great multitude</u>, which no man could number, of all nations, and kindreds, and people, and tongues, stood before the throne, and before the Lamb, clothed with <u>white robes</u>, and palms in their hands;*

10. *And cried with a loud voice, saying, Salvation to our God which sitteth upon the throne, and unto the Lamb.*

11. *And all the angels stood round about the throne, and about the elders, and the four beasts (living creatures), and fell before the throne on their faces, and worshipped God.*

12. *Saying, Amen; Blessing, and glory, and wisdom, and thanksgiving, and honour, and power, and might, be unto our God forever and ever. Amen!* (Emphasis added.)

We see here a multitude of redeemed saints clothed in their eternal 'white robes'. They are worshipping and magnifying God and the Lamb waving palms before His throne. We know they are resurrected because they already had on their eternal garments.

Verses 13-17:

13. *And one of the elders answered, saying unto me, What are these which are arrayed in <u>white robes</u>? and whence came they*

14. *And I said unto him, Sir, thou knowest. And he said to me, These are they which came out of great tribulation, and have washed their robes, and made them white in the blood of the Lamb.*

15. *Therefore are they before the throne of God, and serve him day and night in his temple; and he that sitteth on the throne shall dwell among them.*

16. *They shall hunger no more, neither thirst any more; neither shall the sun light on them, nor any heat.*

17. *For the Lamb which is in the midst of the throne shall feed them, and shall lead them unto living fountains of waters; and God shall wipe away all tears from their eyes.*

WHO ARE THESE?

To make sure that John was getting all that God was showing him in the heavenlies, one of the elders asked him this question. So much was happening so fast, John could only reply, *"Sir, thou knowest!"* When Paul was caught away into the Third Heaven, he saw things that he was not even allowed to tell. We thank God that John was allowed to share with us his heavenly visitation to bring us the events of the end-times.

"These are they which came out of great tribulation!" It does not necessarily mean here that this group came out of that which we call "The Great Tribulation". It was really too soon for them to be in heaven already before the throne of God. This great multitude was the saints of all ages who were now resurrected having been tried upon the earth through persecutions and tribulations. Look at those who were persecuted during the days of Nero and Diocletion.

Look at those who suffered under the cruel hand of Rome during the Dark Ages. What about the Huguenots of France who were so on fire for God that nearly half of France was converted until this group was stopped by Cardinal Richeleau and his cruel persecution. In the massacre of St. Bartholomew, thousands were slaughtered in the name of religion and the Huguenots fled to America and South Africa. All of these are among that great multitude before the throne of God

Because so many of this 'great multitude' had been hurt during their earthly journey, God gives them some very wonderful promises here in this text.

1. *"They shall hunger no more"*
2. *"Neither thirst anymore"*
3. *"Neither shall the sun light on them"*
4. *"Nor any heat"*
5. *"The Lamb shall feed them"*
6. *"And lead them unto living fountains of waters"*
7. *"God shall wipe away all tears from their eyes"*

Imagine what these promises must have meant to them after all their earthly sufferings. Now it was all over and forever they were with the Lamb in His glory. So we leave this parenthetical chapter to continue looking at the opening of the seals. The 'Seventh Seal' is ready to be opened.

CHAPTER 8

THE TRUMPET JUDGEMENTS

Verse 1:

And when he had opened the <u>seventh seal</u>, there was silence in heaven about the space of half an hour.

Somehow, religion has given us the idea that heaven is a quiet, peaceful place where all is serene and silent. Do you know that this verse is the only one that speaks of *"silence'* in heaven? Twenty-five times in the Book of Revelation, it declares that in heaven there will be *"loud voices"* and *"great voices"*, but no *"silence"* except in this verse.

Have you ever been to Niagara Falls at the New York/Canadian border? Or to Victoria Falls in Africa?

Or to Iguazu Falls in Argentina? You can't hear yourself think because of the *"voice of many waters"*. This is what it declares about the worship in heaven for all eternity.

"And I heard a voice from heaven, as the <u>voice of many waters</u>, and as the <u>voice of a great thunder;</u> and I heard the <u>voice of harpers</u> harping with their harps." (Rev. 14:2).

"And after these things, I heard a <u>great voice</u> of much people in heaven, saying, Alleluia!" (Rev. 19:1).

"And I heard as it were the <u>voice of a great multitude</u>, and as the <u>voice of many waters</u>, and as the <u>voice of mighty thunderings</u>, saying, Alleluia!" (Rev. 19:6 emphasis added).

My husband's mother said to me one day, "Why do you Pentecostals always have to make so much noise in church. Don't you know God is not dead?" I thought for a moment, then politely answered, "No, and He is not nervous either!" Whether we like our church worship noisy or quiet is our privilege down here, but it will not be up there. Heaven will be a noisy place of constant worship and praise unto our God so why not get a little used to it here!

What is the reason then for this *"silence"* for this short space of time? I pondered that myself and can only think that the "White horse armies of heaven" were standing at alert and in silence awaiting the word from the "Commander-in-Chief, Jesus" to give the charge to ride to the Battle of Armageddon. This will take place at the very close of the Great Tribulation following the outpouring of the "Wrath of God Almighty". We will see more about it when we get to chapter 19 of Revelation.

Verses 2-6:

2. *And I saw the seven angels which stood before God; and to them were given seven trumpets.*

3. *And another angel came and stood at the altar, having a golden censer; and there was given unto him much incense, that he should offer it with the prayers of all saints upon the golden altar which was before the throne.*

4. *And the smoke of the incense, which came with the prayers of the saints, ascended up before God out of the angel's hand.*

5. *And the angel took the censer, and filled it with fire of the altar, and cast it into the earth; and there were voices, and thunderings, and lightnings, and an earthquake.*

6. *And the seven angels which had the seven trumpets prepared themselves to sound.*

The opening of the Seventh Seal gave way to the Seven Trumpet Judgments and the outpouring of the wrath of Almighty God at the very end of the Tribulation Period of 3 ½ years. The anti-Christ had his day for a short space of time. He came to torment those who had not been ready for the *"catching away"* and to persecute the Jews upon the earth. Remember that God had sealed 144,000 of the Jews so that the anti-Christ could not destroy them.

"Woe unto the inhabitants of the earth and of the sea! For the devil is come down unto you, having great wrath, because <u>he knoweth that he hath but a short time!</u>" (Rev. 12:12).

The "man of sin", the "son of perdition", the "anti-Christ" will have his day for a mere 3 ½ years and then it will be God's turn to judge the earth and the "great whore" (Rev.17,18) which we shall discuss later when we get to those chapters. So now in the rest of Chapter 8, we will look at "The Seven Trumpet Judgments".

Verse 7:

The first angel sounded, and there followed hail and fire mingled with blood, and they were cast upon the earth; and the third part of the trees was burnt up, and all green grass was burnt up.

The First Trumpet Judgment

1. Hail and fire are rained upon the earth.
2. A third part of the trees are burnt up.
3. All the green grass is burnt up as well.

Verses 8,9:

8. And the second angel sounded, and as it were a great mountain burning with fire was cast into the sea; and the third part of the sea became blood.

9. And the third part of the creatures which were in the sea, and had life, died; and the third part of the ships were destroyed.

The Second Trumpet Judgment

1. A great fiery mountain was cast into the sea.
2. A third part of the sea became blood.
3. A third part of the creatures in the sea died.
4. A third part of the ships were destroyed.

As we have taught before, God works in "threes" in keeping with His Divine nature as Father, Word/Son, and Holy Spirit. It seems that even in judgment, He does it by the number three, a third part of each thing.

Verses 10,11:

10. *And the third angel sounded, and there fell a great star from heaven, burning as it were a lamp, and it fell upon the third part of the rivers, and upon the fountains of waters;*

11. *And the name of the star is called Wormwood; and the third part of the waters became wormwood; and many men died of the waters, because they were made bitter.*

The Third Trumpet Judgment

1. A great burning star fell from heaven.
2. It fell upon a third part of rivers and fountains.
3. The star was named "Wormwood" (bitter).
4. It made the waters bitter and people died.

Verse 12:

And the fourth angel sounded, and the third part of the sun was smitten, and the third part of the moon, and the third part of the stars; so as the third part of them was darkened, and the day shone not for a third part of it, and the night likewise.

The Fourth Trumpet Judgment

1. A third part of the sun is smitten.
2. A third part of the moon as well.

3. Also a third part of the stars of heaven.
4. This made a third part of the day to be dark
    and a third part of the night to be light.

Verse 13:

And I beheld, and heard an angel flying through the midst of heaven, saying with a loud voice, Woe, woe, woe to the inhabiters of the earth by reason of the other voices of the trumpet of the three angels which are yet to sound!

In these words, we are brought to Chapter 9 of the Apocalypse where the last three Trumpet Judgments are given from heaven. It will be interesting to note in this study that some of this time of tragedy and judgment has already befallen our own United States in the terrible day of infamy called 9/11. What happened here in our land on that day was just a type and shadow of that which will be coming at the close of the Great Tribulation. Read on in Chapter 9 to see what it's all about.

CHAPTER 9

WHO DID THIS TO US?

We had just arrived back in the U.S. after one of our many overseas trips to the nations with the gospel of our Lord Jesus. We arrived late into the Miami Intl. Airport so had to stay overnight near the airport and take our flight on home to Orlando the next morning. It was the evening of September 10, 2001. We were so tired from the long trip and went to bed right after a little evening meal. About eight in the morning, we awakened and, while my husband was brushing his teeth, I turned on the TV to Fox News. It was about ten minutes 'til nine on the morning of September 11th.

What I saw suddenly on the screen caused me to cry out to Bob, "Come here at once! Something horrible has happened!" And there before our very eyes was the horror of that plane flying into building one of the Twin Towers of the World Trade Center in New York. As we watched in unbelief, we saw the second plane strike the second tower and wondered what would happen next.

My husband, Bob, rushed down to the hotel lobby to see about our flight out that morning. The hotel desk quickly informed us that all flights everywhere had been cancelled and the airport was under tight security. So what about a rental car to drive up to our home? Every car that could be rented was already booked so now what? We called one of our spiritual sons, Pastor Scott, and he rushed right over to the hotel. One of his members had an Avis rental agency so he might still have a car left. Praise God, he had a brand new car not yet into service. It was ours free and to add to our blessing on that infamous day, all of the Florida Turnpike tollbooths were wide open with no tolls being collected.

We were scheduled that Friday night to preach at a city-wide rally up in South Carolina. As it so happened, that day was chosen by President Bush as a day of memorial prayers for the nation so our meeting became a large prayer gathering of all churches in the area at the city auditorium. God gave Bob a message from Revelation 9:11 – "Who Did This To Us?" We will look at that in just a moment, but first, the next Trumpet Judgment.

THE FIFTH ANGEL SOUNDS

Verses 1-10:

1. *And the fifth angel sounded, and I saw a star fall from heaven unto the earth; and to him was given the key of the bottomless pit.*

2. *And he opened the bottomless pit; and there arose a smoke out of the pit, as the smoke of a great furnace; and the sun and the air were darkened by reason of the smoke of the pit.*

3. *And there came out of the smoke locusts upon the earth; and unto them was given power, as the scorpions of the earth have power.*

4. *And it was commanded them that they should not hurt the grass of the earth, neither any green thing, neither any tree; but only those men which have not the seal of God in their foreheads.*

5. *And to them it was given that they should not kill them, but that they should be tormented five months; and their torment was as the torment of a scorpion, when he striketh a man.*

6. *And in those days shall men seek death, and shall not find it; and shall desire to die, and death shall flee from them.*

7. *And the shapes of the locusts were like unto horses prepared unto battle; and on their heads were as it were crowns like gold, and their faces were as the faces of men.*

8. *And they had hair as the hair of women, and their teeth were as the teeth of lions.*

9. *And they had breastplates, as it were breastplates of iron; and the sound of their wings was as the sound of chariots of many horses running to battle.*

10. *And they had tails like unto scorpions, and there were stings in their tails; and their power was to hurt men five months.*

In this first verse, we see *"a star fall from heaven"* and he was given *"the key of the bottomless pit"*. This is a most interesting fact as it helps explain the fall of Lucifer as recorded in Isaiah 14:12-16.

> *"How art thou fallen from heaven, O Lucifer, son of the morning! How art thou cut down to the ground, which didst weaken the nations!*
>
> *For thou hast said in thine heart, I will ascend into heaven, I will exalt my throne above the stars of God; I will sit also upon the mount of the congregation, in the sides of the north.*
>
> *I will ascend above the heights of the clouds; I will be like the Most High God.*
>
> *Yet thou shalt be brought down to hell, to the sides of the pit.*
>
> *They that see thee shall narrowly look upon thee, and consider thee, saying, Is this the man that made the earth to tremble, that did shake kingdoms;*
>
> *That made the world as a wilderness, and destroyed the cities thereof; that opened not the house of his prisoners?"*

In this Fifth Trumpet Judgment, we note two specific things mentioned:

The Bottomless Pit – This is the first mention in Scripture of this place. It is referred to seven times in the Book of Revelation and we learn something about it as we further study.

1. It was like a great furnace and thick smoke arose from it. (9:2).
2. A fallen angel was in charge of it. We know this to be Lucifer, the Prince of Demons. (11:7).
3. The "beast" which is the anti-Christ ascended out of it. We shall see who he really is later in our study. (17:8).
4. An angel came down from heaven having the key to it. (20:1).
5. Satan was bound a thousand years and cast into the Bottomless Pit. (20:3).

Demonic Locusts – The description of these demonic insects was like nothing else ever described in the Word of God.

> They were like tormenting scorpions.
> They were not allowed to kill anyone.
> They were like horses ready for battle.
> They had crowns of gold on their heads.
> Their faces were like the faces of men.
> Their hair was long as women's hair.
> Their teeth were like those of a lion.
> They had breastplates of iron.
> Their wings sounded like chariots.
> Their tails had stingers like scorpions.

In Joel 1:4, the prophet describes the wasting of the land by several insects and included among them is the "locust". In Joel 2:25, God gives a precious promise to His people. *"And I will restore to you the years that the locust hath eaten ..."*

These words of prophecy from God's End time Prophet Joel had to do with the 'restoration' of all things to His Church in the last day. The words in Revelation had to do with the 'destruction' at the end of the Great Tribulation.

We also see in Verse 9 that they had power to hurt men for five months. Why five months? Five is the number of grace and the grace of God is so great that even in tribulation His grace and mercy always exceed His judgment. We have learned through our years of study and ministry that God is like an eternal wheel. His grace and mercy side is always on the top of the wheel while His judgment side is on the bottom. However, when God is fed up, He is fed up and says in so many words, "Enough is enough!"

"For then shall be great tribulation, such as was not since the beginning of the world to this time, no, nor ever shall be. And except those days be shortened (five months), there should no flesh be saved!" (Matt. 24:21,22).

Verses 11,12:

11. *And they had a king over them, which is the angel of the bottomless pit, whose name in the Hebrew tongue is Abaddon, but in the Greek tongue hath his name Apollyon.*

12. *One woe is past; and, behold, there come two woes more hereafter.*

The question at the beginning of this chapter was, "Who Did This To Us?" Now, we have the answer, 'THE DESTROYER'. This is the meaning of both the Hebrew and Greek names for this one from the Bottomless Pit. Of course, he is none other than old Lucifer himself, but thank God, we know his future.

"The thief (which is the devil) cometh not, but for to steal, and to kill, and to destroy" (John 10:10a). This has always been the work of the old enemy. This verse goes on to tell us just the opposite about our wonderful Lord Jesus. *"I am come that they might have life, and that they might have it more abundantly!"* (John 10:10b).

Don't let these "woes" of Revelation get you down because, if you are overcoming in your walk with God, they will have no bearing on you whatsoever. As we find it necessary to study about the end-times and what will happen during the Great Tribulation, take courage and remember what the great Apostle Paul told us in Romans 8:35,37, *"Who shall separate us from the love of Christ? Shall tribulation, or distress, or persecution, or famine, or nakedness, or peril, or sword? Nay, in all these things we are more than conquerors through him that loved us!"*

THE SIXTH ANGEL SOUNDS

Verses 13-21:

13. *And the sixth angel sounded, and I heard a voice from the four horns of the golden altar which is before God,*

14. *Saying to the sixth angel which had the trumpet, Loose the four angels which are bound in the great river Euphrates,*
15. *And the four angels were loosed, which were prepared for an hour, and a day, and a month , and a year, for to slay the third part of men.*

16. *And the number of the army of the horsemen were two hundred thousand thousand, and I heard the number of them.*

17. *And I saw the horses in the vision, and them that sat on them, having breastplates of fire, and of jacinth, and brim-stone; and the heads of the horses were as the heads of lions; and out of their mouths issued fire and smoke and brimstone.*

18. *By these three was the third part of men killed, by the fire, and by the smoke, and by the brimstone, which issued out of their mouths.*

19. *For their power is in their tails; for their tails were like unto serpents, and had heads, and with them they do hurt.*

20. *And the rest of the men which were not killed by these plagues yet repented not of the works of their hands, that they should not worship devils, and idols of gold, and silver, and brass, and stone, and of wood, which neither can see, nor hear, nor walk;*

21. *Neither repented they of their murders, nor of their sorceries, not of their fornication, not of their thefts.*

After studying this chapter, it makes me shiver to think that so many people in these last days (though we do not know the day or the hour when the Lord will come) are going about their own business giving no heed to the times and no time for God. Yet, with all of signs around us, those of the world don't seem to be under any conviction of their sins. God is literally blotted out of their minds. We should tremble as we read the unfolding of Revelation, knowing that we may have relatives or close friends outside the ark of safety.

The voice John hears at the sounding of the Sixth Trumpet comes from the *"four horns of the golden altar which is before God."* This golden altar is found in the *"temple of the tabernacle of the testimony in heaven."* (Rev. 15:5). There was a *"first covenant"* and a *"first tabernacle"* according to Hebrews 9, which gives the entire account of the Tabernacle of Moses which God, gave to him by the pattern he showed Moses in Mount Sinai. This earthly tabernacle was for that time, *"a figure of the time then present"* (Heb. 9:9).

"But Christ being come an high priest of good things to come, by a greater and more perfect tabernacle, not made with hands." (Heb. 9:11).

Here now in Revelation, we see the progression of that Heavenly Tabernacle and this Sixth Angel is in the Holy Place of the Tabernacle of Heaven. The voice comes from the Golden Altar of Incense, which has the four horns on each corner. This altar represents the place of prayer and praise where the High Priest of old offered up incense unto God in petition and in praise. Years ago the saints of God would use the expression when deep in prayer, "Let's get hold of the horns of the altar!" meaning to really get into earnestly seeking God.

Some very terrible things happened at the sounding of this trumpet.

1. Four angels were loosed from the River Euphrates. It is interesting to note that the Euphrates River is spoken of in the Book of Genesis 2:14 as coming out of the Garden of Eden. Today, this river along with the Tigris both flow through the City of Baghdad in Iraq.

2. 200 million horsemen were loosed upon the earth. In pondering this, it is likely that they were demon spirits although it is possible they could be actual horsemen.

3. A third part of humanity was killed upon the earth by this army.

4. The rest who were not killed could have had a chance to change and escape, but it says they *"repented not"*. It makes us wonder how hardened can the hearts of men be.

CHAPTER 10

TIME SHALL BE NO MORE

Verses 1-6:

1. *And I saw another mighty angel come down from heaven, clothed with a cloud; and a rainbow was upon his head, and his face was as it were the sun, and his feet as pillars of fire;*

2. *And he had in his hand a little book open; and he set his right foot upon the sea, and his left foot on the earth.*

3. *And cried with a loud voice, as when a lion roareth; and when he had cried, seven thunders uttered their voices.*

4. *And when the seven thunders had uttered their voices, I was about to write; and I heard a voice from heaven saying unto me, Seal up those things which the seven thunders uttered, and write them not.*

5. *And the angel which I saw stand upon the sea and upon the earth lifted up his hand to heaven.*

6. *And sware by him that liveth forever and ever, who created heaven, and the things that therein are, and the earth, and the things that therein are, and the sea, and the things which are therein, that there should be time no longer.*

This chapter of Revelation is parenthetical to the major events surrounding the Great Tribulation. *"Another angel"* has a part in these end time events. This angel is called here a *"mighty angel"*. In Revelation 5:2, John saw a *"strong angel"*. The meaning of both 'strong' and 'mighty' are basically the same. These angels were powerful, forcible, strong, valiant and mighty. These angels had been greatly tested and had overcome.

I am sure that they were tested during Lucifer's rebellion in heaven back in eternity. There were some angels who cast their lot with Lucifer as he recruited them to follow him. Other angels, like this mighty one, rose up and warred to overcome Lucifer's temptation. We see by this that even angels had to be overcomers.

This strong angel speaking loudly said, *"Who is worthy to open the book and to loose the seals?"* (Rev.5:2). He knew that no one except the Lord of Glory, the Lion who was also the Lamb, He alone was worthy to do this great task. The greatness of this mighty angel was so powerful that he was able to stand with one foot on the land and the other on the sea as he prepared to make a mighty declaration.

As this angel cried with this loud voice, seven thunders uttered and roared from heaven and John must have been amazed at what they uttered. He was about to take out his pen and write, when the Lord stopped him and said, *"Seal up those things ... and write them not!"*

Remember back when Paul was taken up into the 'Third Heaven' that God also told him that he could not reveal what he saw or heard. It appears that there are some secrets of heaven, and probably lots of them, that God will not reveal until that great day when we are with Him for eternity. I believe that heaven is going to be a place of learning and knowledge beyond anything we could ever learn down here with our finite minds. No wonder we can sing, "Won't it be wonderful there having no burdens to bear; joyously singing with harp bells all ringing; oh, won't it be wonderful there!"

John must have seen and heard all he was supposed to for that time, because suddenly the mighty angel declared, *"that there should be time no longer!"*

During our forty years of pastoral ministry, we always looked forward to our great Sunday evening services. They were always alive with the dynamics of the Holy Spirit. The wonderful singing, the anointed special music, the preaching of the Word of God, the great altar calls, O, how we would love to be in some of them now in these days when there are no more Sunday night services in most places. Souls were saved, the sick were healed, seekers were filled with the Holy Spirit and lives were changed.

Many a young person is in the ministry today and serving God on the mission field somewhere because of those great Sunday night evangelistic services. One of our favorite songs from the old 'Melodies of Praise' hymnal was page 182 and how we loved to sing it along with the choir and orchestra.

When the trumpet of the Lord shall sound,
And time shall be no more;
And the morning breaks eternal bright and fair.
When the saved of earth shall gather
Over on the other shore;
And the roll is called up yonder, I'll be there!

This is what we loved to sing about and this is what the text here is telling us, 'Time shall be no more!" God, in His amazing eternal plan, chose to plan time to be sandwiched in between 'eternity past' and 'eternity future'. We were with Him back in eternity and will go back to be with Him in the eternal ages to come.

"That in the <u>ages to come</u> he might shew the exceeding riches of his grace in his kindness toward us through Christ Jesus!" (Eph. 2:7).

God's greatness, His grace and His glory are so vast and profound that is going to take the *"ages to come"* to even begin to understand and comprehend all of Him.

Many years ago we learned a precious chorus that may not be totally correct as far as our doctrine taught us, but the truth of it certainly will be clear to us in that eternal day of God.

Oh, the throne room looks the same
As I ascend back from whence I came;
And the scepter that was mine before I left there.
As I sat with all the sages, I was enthroned with
   throughout the ages;
But most of all my Father out of whom I came.

There was Abraham, Isaac and Jacob;
And Sarah involved in my makeup;
And all the others who were in my family tree.
And down the corridors of eternity,
'Twas God who planned my destiny;
And back into Him I can trace my pedigree.

Eternity past may be hidden from us now, but it will be revealed to us in totality in that great day. The term used in our text here is *"when the mystery of God should be finished"* which, of course, will not be fully revealed until that day when we are with Him forever and ever. One thing we do know and are assured of in the Word:

"He hath chosen us in him before the foundation of the world, that we should be holy and without blame before him in love!" (Eph.1:4).

We, who are the trophies of His grace, have this hope within us that we shall be with Him in 'eternity future' as we were *"chosen in Him"* back in 'eternity past'. This period we call 'time' is for the purpose that God may show to the world *"the riches of the glory of his inheritance in the saints."* (Eph.1:18).

THE LITTLE BOOK

Verses 7-11:

7. *But in the days of the voice of the seventh angel, when he shall begin to sound, the mystery of God should be finished, as he hath declared to his servants the prophets.*

8. *And the voice which I heard from heaven spake unto me again, and said, Go and take the little book which is open in the hand of the angel which standeth upon the sea and upon the earth.*

9. *And I went unto the angel, and said unto him, Give me the little book. And he said unto me, Take it, and eat it up; and it shall make thy belly bitter, but it shall be in thy mouth sweet as honey.*

10. *And I took the little book out of the angel's hand, and ate it up; and it was in my mouth sweet as honey; and as soon as I had eaten it, my belly was bitter.*

11. *And he said unto me, Thou must prophesy again before many peoples, and nations, and tongues, and kings.*

John really had no idea of the contents of "The Little Book", but he wanted to eat of it nonetheless. I had to question why this little book was so sweet to eat like honey, and yet made him have a bellyache after eating it? It is like many things in life that seem so sweet at the time and yet later give us aches and pains. I think that this introduces the inseparable bitter and sweet aspects of our lives in God and of His Word. Many things in the Bible are so precious and sweet and others are very hard to take, yet we need them both.

God starts us out with the cross-life, but the end of His way is resurrection life, glory and eternal exaltation. The Christian walk can sometimes be hard, but it will end in glory when we have overcome. In our text here, the 'sweet part' involves the

Soon-coming King, His millennial kingdom, the New City and His universal reign. The 'bitter part' is God's final judgment and Armageddon.

It is possible that this 'little book' contained the remaining revelation of things yet to come. In other words, everything that would yet transpire in John's disclosure of the Book of Revelation. John received the bitter cup first concerning all the judgments and how bitter it really was. However, the closing chapters of the book leave John with the sweet, sweet taste of the Second Coming of Christ with His White-horse Armies. They let him taste the honey-sweetness of the Holy City and all of its beauty and glory. You may say, but the sweet was supposed to come first and then the bitter. God so many times does things by His own sovereign will and to us it may look like 'the cart before the horse'.

We always remember David Wilkerson's words from his famous vision that God gave him back in the early seventies, 'GOD HAS EVERYTHING UNDER CONTROL!'

CHAPTER 11

THE GREAT TRIBULATION

As we proceed further into the Book of Revelation, we are currently partaking of the very prophecy, which the angel declared, *"Thou must prophesy again before many peoples, and nations, and tongues, and kings."* Chapter 11 records the results of this *"prophesying again"*.

Verses 1,2:

1. *And there was given me a reed like unto a rod; and the angel stood, saying, Rise, and measure the temple of God, and the altar, and them that worship therein.*

2. *But the court which is without the temple leave out, and measure it not; for it is given unto the Gentiles; and the holy city shall they tread under foot forty and two months (3 ½ years).*

In this chapter, John's vision continues on the earth. He is commissioned and equipped to perform a judicial act of measurement of the temple, the altar and those who worship there. God has a specific purpose for this measuring. It was to ascertain the size of the temple and the altar, then to determine the stature and growth of those who worshipped there. This was so He could reward them accordingly. God measures the acts of the righteous, but also those of the wicked so that He might give to everyone their proper reward.

Understand that the anti-Christ, as he comes into power, will ultimately set himself up in this temple and act as though he is God.

"Let no man deceive you by any means; for that day (of Christ's coming) shall not come, except there come a falling away first, and that man of sin be revealed, the son of perdition; Who opposeth and exalteth himself above all that is called God, or that is worshipped; so that he as God sitteth in the temple of God, shewing himself that he is God!" (2 Thess. 2:3,4).

Wow! What blasphemy and brazenness that this usurper, the anti-Christ, really has! He will be an imposter and an imitator. He will usurp God's temple and altar for a short season, namely 3 ½ years.

We go on to see that the outer court was not to be measured because it was given to the Gentiles to be trodden under foot for a period of forty-two months or 3 ½ years. In this short period of time, during which the anti-Christ is given a little season to try to take the place of God, we finally see God's wrath poured out at the very end of the Great Tribulation.

With the introduction of Chapter 11, we see the true length of time of the 'Tribulation Period' which is only 3 ½ years. All our lives, since knowing Christ, including our teachings at Bible College, we were taught that the Tribulation was seven years in length. Now, in my exhaustive studies of Revelation, I could not even find a 'Seven-year period of Tribulation' mentioned in the Book of Revelation. There are lots of 'sevens' in the Apocalypse, but none of them refer to 'Seven years of Tribulation'. So then, where do we get this teaching that the Great Tribulation is seven years?

DANIEL'S SEVENTY WEEKS

It is taken from a faulty interpretation of the Book of Daniel, the ninth chapter, concerning Daniel's vision of 'Seventy weeks'.

"Seventy weeks are determined upon thy people and upon thy holy city to 1) finish the transgression; 2) and to make an end of sins; 3) and to make reconciliation for iniquity; 4) and to bring in everlasting righteousness; 5) and to seal up the vision and prophecy; 6) and to anoint the Most Holy!" (Dan. 9:24).

We must note that all of the six things mentioned here had to do with Jesus, the Messiah, and not the anti-Christ. It was Jesus who *"made an end of sins"* through His own death of the cross. It was Jesus who *"made reconciliation for iniquity"* for Isaiah 53:5 clearly tells us, *"He was wounded for our transgressions, he was bruised for our iniquities; the chastisement of our peace was upon him; and with his stripes we are healed!"*

It was Jesus who came to *"bring in everlasting righteousness"* and it was Jesus who fulfilled all prophecy and truly became the *"anointed Most Holy"*. Daniel 9:26 goes on to say more about this precious Messiah when the prophet declares, *"And after threescore and two weeks shall Messiah be cut off, but not for Himself!"*

Catch this statement, *"not for Himself!"* Of course not, because Jesus never did anything for 'Himself', but always for others, for us. Then the prophecy goes on to say about this wonderful Messiah, *"And he shall confirm the covenant with many for one week (seven years); and in the midst of the week, he shall cause the sacrifice and oblation to cease, and for the over-spreading of abominations, he shall make it desolate!"* (Dan.9:27, emphasis added).

We have been taught that this refers to the anti-Christ when the whole context is about the ministry of the Messiah, Jesus Christ, who definitely was *"cut off"* of His earthly ministry after 3 ½ years or as it says here, *"in the middle of the week"*.

So let's look what we have here in the text of Daniel 9. Jesus has His earthly ministry of 3½ years and is *"cut off"* by His untimely death. When He hangs on the cross, a miraculous thing happens. *"The veil of the temple is rent in twain from the top to the bottom."* (Matt. 27:51). By this one mighty act of Almighty God, the Old Testament *"sacrifice and oblation ceased"* just like Daniel had prophesied. We must note also that Daniel prophesied there would be an *"abomination of desolation"*. This came to pass when they sewed up the veil that God had deliberately torn, and continued on with the sacrifice of animals instead of accepting the sacrifice of God's Only Begotten Son.

"Neither by the blood of goats and calves, but by his own blood, he entered in once into the holy place, having obtained eternal redemption for us!" (Heb. 9:12).

> Jesus paid it all; all to Him I owe;
> Sin had left a crimson stain;
> He washed it white as snow!

One of the saddest statements in God's Word is when the High Priest of Israel said these incredible words recorded in Matthew 27:25, *"Let His (Jesus) blood be upon us and on our children!"*

Even an outsider, a Roman Gentile, knew better than to make such a statement lest he be wrong. Pilate, whose wife was warned in a dream of the innocence of our Lord Jesus, made this statement to the Jewish leaders, *"I am innocent of the blood of this just person (Jesus); see ye to it!"* (Matt. 27:24).

How the Jewish people have gone through untold suffering because of the rejection of their Messiah. Dispersed among the nations, hated by nearly everyone, persecuted over the centuries, and then, the terrible "Holocaust" massacre of over six million Jewish people including innocent men, women and children, all because of their rejection of the One who came to save them, their Messiah.

"He came unto His own (the Jewish people), and his own received Him not. But as many as received Him (Jews and Gentiles), to them gave He power to become the sons of God, even to them that believe on His name!" (John 1:11,12).

One last look at Daniel 9:26 concerning *"a people and a prince that shall come and destroy the city and the sanctuary."* Who was this and when did it happen? If you have studied at all about the great destruction of Jerusalem and the Temple sitting so proudly on that mount, you would know it happened in 70 A.D. under Titus who was a 'prince' in the Roman Empire. The city was destroyed, the temple was destroyed, the Jews were dispersed among the nations and thus we see the fulfillment of Daniel 9.

There are two verses in Daniel that state a period of time in which the anti-Christ will be upon the earth:

"And he (anti-Christ) shall speak great words against the Most High and shall wear out the saints of the Most High, and think to change times and laws; and they shall be given into his hand until a time and times and dividing of a time (3 ½ years)." (Dan. 7:25).

"It shall be for a time, times, and a half (3 ½ years); and when he shall have accomplished to scatter the power of the holy people, all these things shall be finished." (Dan. 12:7).

Both of these verses declare the time of the anti-Christ is to be 3 ½ years! This, plus the six times in the Book of Revelation, the 'Tribulation' is declared to be 3 ½ years, but not even once is seven years mentioned.

This should be proof enough of the length of 'The Great Tribulation'. *"Forty and two months (3 ½ years)"* (Rev. 11:2).

The Holy City trodden under the feet of the Gentiles. *"A thousand two hundred and threescore days (3 ½ yrs)"* (Rev. 11:3).

The Two Witnesses prophesy upon the earth. "*A thousand two hundred and threescore days (3 ½ yrs)*" (Revelation 12:6).

The 'woman' is fed in the wilderness. "*A short time (3 ½ years)*" (Rev.12:12).

Satan's time to try those who dwell upon the earth. "*Time, times, and half a time (3 ½ years)*" (Rev. 12:14).

The 'woman' is preserved from the face of the serpent. "*Forty and two months (3 ½ years)*" (Rev. 13:5).

Power given to the anti-Christ upon the earth.

THE TIMES OF THE GENTILES

"*Jerusalem shall be trodden down of the Gentiles, until the times of the Gentiles be fulfilled.*" (Luke 21:24).

"*For I would not, brethren, that ye should be ignorant of this mystery, lest ye should be wise in your own conceits; that blindness in part is happened to Israel, until the fullness of the Gentiles be come in!*" (Rom. 11:25).

"*How that God had opened the door of faith unto the Gentiles.*" (Acts 14:27).

"*Simeon hath declared how God ...did visit the Gentiles to take out of them a people for his name.*" (Acts 15:14).

"*Be it known therefore unto you, that the salvation of God is sent unto the Gentiles, and that they will hear it!*" (Acts 28:28).

After the first 3 ½ years of Daniel's vision, which was the years of Jesus' earthly ministry, a major change took place in God's economy. Because of Israel's rejection of their Messiah, THE DOOR WAS OPENED TO THE GENTILES! Thus, the world entered what is known in theology as 'The Gentile Age' – 'The Church Age' – 'The Grace Age' or any other name we may want to give it. This time in which we now live is a parenthetical time of God's eternal goodness in the which He has opened His arms to all people everywhere that they might be saved.

Now, let's summarize what we have learned about the Great Tribulation and its length of 3 ½ years:

1. Jesus ministry was 3 ½ years in length that was the first half of Daniel's week.

2. Then came the parenthetical period of time which is now some 2,000 years in which the door of salvation was opened to the Gentiles along with the believing Jews and *'whosoever will'* that might come to the Lord Jesus.

3. This time is coming to a close and the second half of Daniel's week will begin one of these days at the ushering in of the anti-Christ and his reign of 3 ½ years upon this old world and its inhabitants.

I trust that this helps you understand the vision of Daniel upon which the 'Seven-year Tribulation' theory is based.

Verses 3-12:

3. And I will give power unto <u>my two witnesses</u>, and they shall prophecy a thousand two hundred and threescore days (3 ½ years), clothed in sackcloth.

4. These are the two olive trees, and the two candlesticks standing before the God of the earth.

5. And if any man will hurt them, fire proceedeth out of their mouth, and devoureth their enemies; and if any man will hurt them, he must in this manner be killed.

6. These have power to shut heaven, that it rain not in the days of their prophecy; and have power over waters to turn them to blood, and to smite the earth with all plagues, as often as they will.

7. And when they shall have finished their testimony, the beast that ascendeth out of the bottomless pit shall make war against them, and shall overcome them, and kill them.

8. And their dead bodies shall lie in the street of the great city, which spiritually is called Sodom and Egypt, where also our Lord was crucified.

9. And they of the people and kindreds and tongues and nations shall see their dead bodies three days and an half, and shall not suffer their dead bodies to be put in graves.

10. And they that dwell upon the earth shall rejoice over them, and make merry, and shall send gifts one to another, because these two prophets tormented them that dwelt on the earth.

11. And after three days and an half the Spirit of Life from God entered into them, and they stood upon their feet; and great fear fell upon them which saw them.

12. And they heard a great voice from heaven saying unto them, Come up hither. And they ascended up to heaven in a cloud; and their enemies beheld them.

THE TWO WITNESSES

Here is another portion of Revelation, which has been interpreted in various ways. Some commentaries say that the two witnesses are definitely Enoch and Elijah. Others will be emphatic they are Moses and Elijah. Those who would spiritualize most of the Book of Revelation will tell you these 'Two Witnesses' are the Old and New Testaments which witness to Christ upon the earth. Even others say that they will be two witnesses whom God Himself will choose in the end times and no one knows who they will be. Who and what is right is not always easy to discern.

The most common and probably right theory is that these 'Two Witnesses' of whom we have just read will be Enoch and

Elijah. The reasoning is simply this. God's Word says in Hebrews 9:27, *"And as it is appointed unto men once to die, but after this the judgment."* Enoch and Elijah never died an earthly death. Both of them were 'raptured' or 'caught up' into heaven by the Lord. Hence, they must return to earth, fulfill this Scripture, and physically die. This is sound reasoning!

The other theory taught by many is that these two must be Moses and Elijah as they were the two with Jesus on the Mount of Transfiguration.

"And after six days Jesus taketh Peter, James, and John his brother, and bringeth them up into an high mountain apart. And was transfigured before them; and his face did shine as the sun, and his raiment was white as the light. And, behold, there appeared unto them MOSES and ELIJAH talking with him. Then answered Peter, and said unto Jesus, Lord, it is good for us to be here; if thou wilt, let us make here three tabernacles; one for thee, and one for MOSES, and one for ELIJAH!" (Matt. 17:1-4).

Here we have the representation of the law in Moses, the prophets in Elijah, and grace and truth in Jesus. In Luke 16:16 we read, *"The law and the prophets were until John (the Baptist); since that time the Kingdom of God is preached, and every man presseth into it!"*

Taking these strong Scriptures, it could well be the 'Two Witnesses' are none other than Moses and Elijah. Like one news media outlet declares, "We report, you decide!" It really does not make any difference because it is not who they are, but rather what they are doing that makes the difference.

These 'Two Witnesses' are referred to in prophecy as found in Zechariah 4 where God speaks saying, *"Not by might, nor by power, but by my Spirit, saith the Lord of hosts."* The prophet then describes the 'Two Witnesses' and says, *"These are the two anointed ones that stand by the Lord of the whole earth!"*

People who have read about these 'Two Witnesses' down through time, have wondered how such a thing could be that the whole world could know about their witnessing and their dead bodies lying in the street of Jerusalem after God allows them to be killed.

"And their dead bodies shall lie in the street of the great city, which spiritually is called Sodom and Egypt, where also our Lord was crucified. And they of the people and kindreds and tongues and nations shall see their dead bodies three days and an half." (Rev. 11:8,9).

With the telecommunications of today, the whole world can see anything going on almost anywhere and at any time. Only in these last days could this Scripture possibly be fulfilled and it will be during the time of the Great Tribulation.

Our God is so wise and mighty that He has devised a plan to get the attention of the nations as to His mighty power. He allows His witnesses to be slain and lets their dead bodies lie in the street with the entire world's news media people broadcasting this strange phenomenon. Then, suddenly, God breathes life back into them and they stand upon their feet. People around the world are talking and wondering when suddenly something else takes place. *"They ascended up to heaven in a cloud; and their enemies beheld them!"*

God has attracted the attention of the nations, even those who do not believe there is a God or those who think God is someone besides the One and Only Jehovah God. He goes on to add a little more fanfare to the story of His 'Two Witnesses'.

Verses 13,14:

13. *And the same hour was there a great earthquake, and the tenth part of the city fell, and in the earthquake were slain of men seven thousand; and the remnant were affrighted, and gave glory to the God of heaven.*

14. *The second woe is past; and, behold, the third woe cometh quickly.*

Now, God sends a mighty earthquake, which takes the lives of some seven thousand in the City of Jerusalem. God has the attention of the nations as all news media is now focusing on this unusual end-time event God is orchestrating. The Seventh Angel is getting ready to sound his trumpet and God wants the world to hear what the trumpet sound is declaring.

Verses 15-19:

15. *And the seventh angel sounded; and there were great voices in heaven, saying, The kingdoms of this world are become the kingdoms of our Lord, and of his Christ; and he shall reign forever and ever.*

16. *And the four and twenty elders, which sat before God on their seats, fell upon their faces, and worshipped God.*

17. *Saying, We give thee thanks, O Lord God Almighty, which art, and wast, and art to come; because thou hast taken to thee thy great power, and hast reigned.*

18. *And the nations were angry, and thy wrath is come, and the time of the dead, that they should be judged, and that thou shouldest give reward unto thy servants the prophets, and to the saints, and them that fear thy name, small and great; and shouldest destroy them which destroy (corrupt) the earth.*

19. *And the temple of God was opened in heaven, and there was seen in his temple the ark of his testament; and there were lightnings, and voices, and thunderings, and an earthquake, and great hail."*

These present the 'Hallelujah Chorus' from Handel's Messiah are forever words sung by great choirs every Christmas Season as they true.

"And He shall reign forever and ever!"

The message of verse 15 was implanted on the heart of George Gredrick Handel and motivated him to pen a major portion of his oratorio, "The Messiah" in the Hallelujah

Chorus". It always stirs my own heart to hear the mass choirs sing these marvelous word, *"And He shall reign forever and ever!"* In verses 16 and 17, the 24 Elders once again fall down in worship unto the Lord of Lords who sits upon the Eternal Throne of Glory.

Verse 18 looks ahead to the Great White Throne of God revealed in Revelation 20, which we will study in detail. God has great rewards for all those who serve Him and His righteous judgment for those who have rebelled against Him.

Finally, in chapter 11, we see the great temple of God opened in heaven and there was revealed the *"ark of the testimony"*. In this eternal ark, which we see so often in the Old Testament and again spoken of in Hebrews chapter 9. In this beautiful golden ark covered by the mercy seat of God and the cherubim of His glory, were found the tables of the commandments, which the Father had given to Moses on Mount Sinai. Also, inside this ark was the pot of manna and Aaron's rod that budded. Now it was opened in plain view in the Heavenly Temple for the redeemed to see it in all of its glory. Maybe you remember that in the Bible days only the High Priest could look at it and then only once a year.

God gave a little glimpse of His wonderful grace when He allowed it to be brought up to Mount Zion by David, His anointed servant. David danced before it with all his might and worshipped the Lord there on the mountain in the Tabernacle of David, the tent that he had erected for it. There was not a veil to cover it and the Glory of the Shekinah was upon it day and night. What a picture of the eternal glory that we shall be in through eternity.

CHAPTER 12

A GREAT WONDER IN HEAVEN

Verses 1,2,5:

1. *And there appeared a great wonder in heaven; a woman clothed with the sun, and the moon under her feet, and upon her head a crown of twelve stars;*

2. *And she being great with child cried, travailing in birth, and pained to be delivered.*

5. *And she brought forth a manchild, who was to rule all nations with a rod of iron; and her child was <u>caught up</u> unto God, and to his throne."* (Emphasis added.)

I deliberately skipped Verses 3 and 4 for now as they are parenthetical in this setting. We will address them in a moment.

THE WOMAN AND THE MANCHILD

We have come to one of the greatest argumentative Scriptures in the entire Bible. The 'Woman and the Manchild', who are they? After much prayer, study and searching many manuscripts, I have come to the only conclusion I can find that I may be *"rightly dividing the Word of Truth!"* (2 Tim. 2:15).

First, let me share with you an experience we had with this 'woman' mentioned in our text being surrounded with *"the sun ... the moon ... the stars"*.

On one of our many trips to the Holy Land, we visited the largest and most beautiful church in the entire Middle East. It is located in Nazareth where our Jesus grew up. In the lower part of this magnificent structure is a small, ancient grotto where it is supposed that the Virgin Mary was visited by the angel Gabriel and received the annunciation that she was to bear a son and call His name Jesus.

All around the interior of this sanctuary were statues of the Virgin representing different nations of the world and how they viewed her. The one that was the most unusual came from Japan where she was presented as a beautiful young Japanese girl. The most unusual thing about this church, however, was the vast painting high up in the ceiling. How anyone could get that high up to create such a vast painting is hard to understand, but there it was.

Father God was upon a huge central throne. On His right hand was a smaller throne whereon was seated our Lord Jesus. On the other side of the central throne was another throne with a cloud somewhat surrounding it. This represented the Holy Spirit, I am sure. Above all of this was another fourth throne. Seated on this throne was the Virgin Mary, co-redemptress of heaven (according to their theology). She was *"clothed with the sun, the moon was under her feet, and on her head was a crown of twelve stars."* There is no question to the identity of this 'woman' of Revelation 12, according to the Roman Catholic Church. It had to be the Virgin Mary!

The general teaching of evangelicals is that this 'woman' is Israel and the 'manchild' is the Lord Jesus. This theory is taken from the fact that Jesus *"came unto His own"*, the Jewish people, so Israel must indeed be the 'woman'. They teach that Jesus must be the 'manchild' because He is the only one who could *"rule with a rod of iron"*. Let me disprove that right here.

First, we are looking at *"things which must shortly come to pass!"* This was written many, many years after either the Virgin Mary or Israel could have brought forth the Lord Jesus.

In other words, these facts were historical not futuristic. Then, we find a wonderful promise to the 'overcomers' given to those who *"overcame by the blood of the Lamb and the word of their testimony"*.

"And he that overcometh, and keepeth my works unto the end, to him will I give power over the nations; And he shall rule them with a rod of iron!" (Rev. 2:26,27, emphasis added).

Yes, our Lord Jesus will *"rule with a rod of iron"*, but *so will those who are overcomers!* It is plainly written here to the Church of Thyatira and to us in our day.

We also see from our text that the 'woman' was in heaven, not on earth, so this eliminates both the Virgin Mary and Israel for they were both on the earth when Jesus came forth. So, now we see that this 'woman' cannot be the Virgin Mary and she cannot be Israel. *Who is she?* I believe that this 'woman' is the Universal Church who bears the name of Christ throughout the earth. Out of this Church Universal comes forth an 'overcoming company', which the Word of God here calls *"the manchild"*.

THE WOMAN = THE CHURCH

Jesus clearly taught in His earthly ministry concerning 'The Church'. He said these words in Matthew 16:18, *"I (Jesus) will build My Church, and the gates of hell shall not prevail against it!"* (Emphasis added.)

Down through the centuries of time, 'The Church' has been fought more than any other organization or entity, but she still prevails. The floods could not drown it; the fires could not burn it; the winds could not destroy it; and the Church of Jesus Christ still stands strong in the earth today in spite of her many weaknesses. I believe that this 'woman' of Revelation 12 is that Church!

Now, it is true that the Church Universal is not always the purest or most perfect example of Jesus or the Father. She has made countless mistakes down through the ages, but almost always it was the men who dominated the Church that were in error. Yet, within her walls were the hungry and thirsty that Jesus taught about. *"Blessed are they which do hunger and thirst after righteousness; for they shall be filled!"* (Matt.5:6).

The Church began with all of the Apostolic power given her by the Lord Jesus. Little by little, through the pollution of men's ideas and doctrines, she began to weaken and become polluted. It didn't happen all at once anymore than it does today. We may say, "Oh, we've become enlightened and don't need that old-time religion anymore!", but be careful! We used to sing that old gospel chorus:

> Give me that old time religion,
> Give me that old time religion,
> Give me that old time religion;
> It's good enough for me!
> It was good for our fathers;
> It was good for our mothers;
> It was good for everybody,
> And it's good enough for me!

In the days of Sister Aimee McPherson at Angelus Temple, she taught on the decline of the Church, but also added the restoration of the Church in the last days. In one of her great illustrated sermons, she had an old-fashioned carrousel set up on the platform. She proudly rode the great white stallion around and around. Little by little, the carrousel slowed down and the bright lights dimmed down. Then, suddenly, the whole contraption stopped and the lights went out. All of this was done to the then-popular tune, "The Merry-go-Round Broke Down". Her illustration was that the Church had been beautiful, full of light and constantly moving, but down through the ages the Church slowed down and the lights went dim. Now, in the last days God was going to restore the Church and, once again, the glory would shine in the earth. What a message and what a truth!

The 'woman' is the Church who has made it since its inception by Christ even though stained with errors and problems, but still honored by the Father as she is depicted here in Revelation 12.

"Clothed with the sun" - The *"Sun of righteousness"* who is the Lord Jesus Christ is the covering for His Church. (Mal. 4:2). The glory of the sun is the exaltation of the Church.

"The moon under her feet" – The moon speaks of the night seasons through which the Church must go. It is the humiliation of the Church.

"A crown of twelve stars" – This crown of twelve stars speaks of ruling. That His Church would rule in the earth was the Father's will. In Jesus pattern prayer, He said these words that we all have prayed so many times, *"Thy kingdom come, thy will be done, in earth as it is in heaven!"*

THE MANCHILD = THE OVERCOMERS

Out of the 'Universal Church' will come the remnant, the elect, the overcomers who have let nothing stand in their way from worshipping, serving and loving God. This company of overcomers has been called by many different names down through the years. Some call it 'The Bridal Company'. Others have said it is 'The Manifested Sons of God'. We have heard the overcomers called 'The Elijah Company'. 'The Select of the Elect' is what one preacher called them. Whatever name you may give to those who are the overcomers, they are, nonetheless, 'The Manchild' of Revelation 12. Along with the Lord Jesus, they will someday *"rule with a rod of iron!"* (Revelation 2:27).

THE GREAT RED DRAGON

Verses 3,4:

3. *And there appeared another wonder in heaven; and behold a great red dragon, having seven heads and ten horns, and seven crowns upon his heads.*

4. *And his tail drew the third part of the stars of heaven, and did cast them to the earth; and the dragon stood before the woman which was ready to be delivered, for to devour her child as soon as it was born.*

Sounds like some kind of Chinese mystery story – 'The Great Red Dragon'. Oh, it is a mystery alright, but the Word of God clearly explains who this dragon is and what he is trying to do.

There is no question as to the identity of this 'dragon'. He is none other than fallen Lucifer. We will read more about this later on in this chapter. There are four major names given in God's Word to this fallen angel.

"And he (angel) laid hold on the <u>dragon</u>, that old <u>serpent</u>, which is the <u>Devil</u>, and <u>Satan</u>, and bound him a thousand years." (Rev. 20:2, emphasis added).

1) The Dragon – This is Lucifer's highest form of wickedness. He is called in our text *"the red dragon"* because 'red' denotes his fury and lashing out against the woman, the Church.

2) The Serpent – Another name in the Scriptures for the serpent is 'Leviathan'. Isaiah 27:1 says, *"In that day the Lord with his sore and great and strong sword shall punish <u>leviathan</u> the piercing <u>serpent</u>, even <u>leviathan</u> that crooked <u>serpent</u>; and he shall slay the <u>dragon</u> that is in the sea."* (Emphasis added.)

In the next chapter of Revelation, the beast, who is the anti-Christ, rises up out of the sea in the full fury of Lucifer.

3) The Devil – *"Woe to the inhabitants of the earth and of the sea! For the <u>devil</u> is come down unto you, having great wrath, because he knoweth that he hath but a short time (3 ½ years)."*

The Devil is blamed for lots of things and he is guilty of most of them and is to be blamed. For a while during the 'T-shirt' craze, people were wearing them with the slogan 'The Devil Made Me Do It!' Maybe he did, maybe he didn't! Jesus said these words about this our enemy, *"The thief (the devil) cometh not, but for to steal, and to kill, and to destroy; I am come that they might have life, and that they might have it more abundantly."* (John 10:10).

4) Satan – His name means 'the attacker', 'the resister' and 'the adversary'. Jesus said in the three synoptic Gospels, *"Get thee behind Me, Satan!"*

"Be sober, be vigilant, because your <u>adversary the devil</u>, as a roaring lion, walketh about, seeking whom he may devour; Whom resist stedfast in the faith!" (1 Pet. 5:8,9).

We have seen the whole scene: The woman, the man-child and the red dragon. This is quite a story, which will unfold in the last days during the time of the Tribulation period of 3 ½ years.

Verse 6:

And the woman fled into the wilderness, where she hath a place prepared of God, that they should feed her there a thousand two hundred and threescore days (3 ½ years).

God, in His great mercy and not willing that any should perish, has provided a place where those who had not overcome to make the rapture, but would not take the 'mark of the beast', could find refuge during this time of Great Tribulation. Some have said that this place is 'Petra' out in the hills of Jordan. We have been there on our tours to the Holy Land and it is just too obvious. The anti-Christ would never be fooled by such a place. Even Indiana Jones found Petra in the movie, "The Last Crusade". The Bible does not tell us the location of this 'wilderness' so we cannot just speculate on that which the Scriptures do not clearly tell.

We have learned through the years that speculating on certain portions of Scripture that are difficult to understand can lead into false interpretation and even into false doctrine if carried too far.

THE ENEMY IS DEFEATED!

Verses 7-12:

7. *And there was war in heaven: Michael and his angels fought against the dragon; and the dragon fought and his angels,*

8. *And prevailed not; neither was their place found any more in heaven.*

9. *And the great <u>dragon</u> was cast out, that old <u>serpent</u>, called the <u>Devil</u>, and <u>Satan</u>, which deceiveth the whole world; he was cast out into the earth, and his angels were cast out with him.*

10. *And I heard a loud voice saying in heaven, Now is come salvation, and strength, and the kingdom of our God, and the power of his Christ; for the accuser of our brethren is cast down, which accused them before our God day and night.*

11. *And they overcame him by the blood of the Lamb, and the word of their testimony; and they loved not their lives unto the death.*

12. *Therefore rejoice, ye heavens, and ye that dwell in them. Woe to the inhabitants of the earth and of the sea! For the devil is come down unto you, having great wrath, because he knoweth that he hath but a short time (3 ½ years).*

"War in heaven" - It happened somewhere in the distant past and old Lucifer was cast out and a third of the angels that rebelled with him. Jude 6 says, *"And the angels which kept not*

their first estate, but left their own habitation, he hath reserved in everlasting chains under darkness unto the judgment of the great day."

It appears back in God's eternity the angels were divided into three categories with an appointed archangel over them. This was not unlike God's own eternal triune nature and the way God made humanity as a tri-partite being having spirit, soul and body.

1. The Worshippers – *Lucifer* was the chief archangel of worship before his fall. We have found, even to this day, the enemy fights the worshippers of the Lord because he hates anyone who has taken the place he once had.

2. The Proclaimers – *Gabriel* is the one who brings God's proclamations to the earth. The Lord sent Gabriel to the Prophet Daniel to proclaim to him about the visions he was receiving from the Lord including the vision of 'The Seventy Weeks'. Gabriel appeared unto the Virgin Mary to tell her she would be the honored one to bear His Only Begotten Son into this world.

3. The Warriors – *Michael* was the archangel God sent to do warfare on the earth. When the Prince of Persia withstood Daniel for twenty-one days, Daniel declared, *"Lo, Michael, one of the chief princes (archangels), came to help me!"* (Dan. 10:13

    In Daniel's prophetic word about the end-time, the prophet said this in Daniel 12:1. It clearly speaks of the time of the 'Great Tribulation', *"And at that time shall Michael stand up, the great prince (archangel) which standeth for the children of thy people; and there shall be a time of trouble, such as never was since there was a nation even to that same time; and at that time, thy people shall be delivered, every one that shall be found written in the book (the Lamb's Book of Life)."*

The Bible tells us more about Michael as the warrior, *"Yet Michael the archangel, when contending with the devil, he disputed about the body of Moses."* (Jude 9).

In our text, in Revelation 12:7 it tells us the archangel Michael fought the war in the heavenlies and, of course, we know that he won.

Old 'slewfoot' is still *"the accuser of the brethren"*, but he has been cast down and can only tell lies against us because there is no truth in him. He was a liar from the beginning. Don't let Satan accuse you, even of the things you have done in the past that may not have been pleasing to God. If they are under the blood of Christ through true repentance, they cannot be used against you. Satan loves to roll up his sleeves, reach down into the fountain of Jesus' blood, and drag up your past. God's Word in Psalm 103:10-12 says a big 'NO' to the devil when he tries to do this to us.

"He hath not dealt with us after our sins; nor rewarded us according to our iniquities. For as the heaven is high above the earth, so great is his mercy toward them that fear him. As far as the east is from the west, so far hath he removed our transgressions from us!"

OVERCOMING THE ENEMY

From the very beginning of our study in Revelation, we have seen that the key word of the Book is 'OVERCOME' and the promises are to overcomers.

Revelation 12:11 gives us the *three important ways* in which we can overcome the enemy. This is important because if we are to escape the coming wrath of God upon the sin of this old world, then we must be in that company of 'overcoming saints'.

1. *The Blood of the Lamb* – Nothing is more powerful than the blood of Jesus Christ, God's Son.

"If we walk in the light, as he is in the light, we have fellowship one with another, and <u>the blood of Jesus Christ his Son</u> cleanseth us from ALL SIN!" (1 John 1:7).

> There is power, power wonderworking power
> In the blood of the Lamb.
> There is power, power wonderworking power
> In the precious blood of the Lamb.

2. *The Word of our Testimony* – In our early days in the Pentecostal Movement, we always had those 'testimony meetings' on Sunday night. People would share the wonderful things that God had done for them and the church would be edified. In more recent years, we have not taken time for these testimonies any longer and I fear that we are missing a special time of praise to God for His goodness.

   "By faith Enoch was translated that he should not see death; and was not found, because God had translated him; for before his translation <u>he had this testimony</u> that he pleased God." (Heb.11:5).

3. *Loving not our own lives* – This does not mean that we should not take care of our bodies, but that all we have should not be heaped upon ourselves. Too many times in this life, we try to please the flesh and ignore what God really is wanting of us. Living a 'crucified life' such as Paul described in Galatians 2:20 is not a popular message in today's church, *"I am crucified with Christ; nevertheless I live; yet not I, but Christ liveth in me; and the life which I now live in the flesh I live by the faith of the Son of God, who loved me, and gave himself for me."*

   This was my dad's favorite verse and many times he would share it as he gave his testimony in the church. The Apostle Paul said, *"For me to live is Christ, and to die is gain!"*

(Phil. 1:21). This is what is meant by 'loving not our own lives'.

THE AGE-OLD BATTLE STILL RAGES

Verses 13-17:

13. *And when the dragon saw that he was cast unto the earth, he persecuted the woman which brought forth the manchild.*

14. *And to the woman were given two wings of a great eagle, that she might fly into the wilderness, into her place, where she is nourished for a time, and times, and half a time (3 ½ years) from the face of the serpent.*

15. *And the serpent cast out of his mouth water as a flood after the woman, that he might cause her to be carried away of the flood.*

16. *And the earth helped the woman, and the earth swallowed up the flood which the dragon cast out of his mouth.*

17. *And the dragon was wroth with the woman, and went to make war with the remnant of her seed, which keep the commandments of God, and have the testimony of Jesus Christ!*

The age-old battle still rages between the dragon, called also here the serpent, and the 'woman' who is the Church. and *"the remnant of her seed"*. When old Lucifer, called the dragon and the serpent, was cast out of heaven to the earth, one of his first acts was to beguile the first woman and cause her to fall and her husband, Adam, with her.

"And the serpent said to the woman, Ye shall not surely die ... And when the woman saw that the tree was good for food, and that it was pleasant to the eyes, and a tree to be desired to make one wise, she took of the fruit thereof, and did eat, and gave also to her husband with her, and he did eat!" (Gen. 3:4,6).

It is quite evident that Mr. Adam was with Mrs. Adam and they both ate together of the forbidden fruit being enticed by the serpent. Down through history, fallen Lucifer has badgered and persecuted the Church of Jesus Christ so it will be no different in the end-times.

We see that the woman in our text was taken out into the wilderness where God in His grace and mercy covered her with His Divine protection. The Song of Songs talks about this woman coming up out of the wilderness. *"Who is this that cometh up from the wilderness, leaning upon her beloved? (Song of Songs 8:5).*

The earthly journey of Christ's beloved Bride has always been and always will be a wilderness journey. It is one thing to sit in church thinking all is well with your soul, but it is another thing to be ready when Jesus comes. Those church members, though believers in Christ, were not ready for His coming and have been left to go through the Tribulation. God in His great mercy helps them in this hour of need so they need not take the 'mark of the beast'. Now, they know they missed it and greatly fear the Lord. Psalm 103:13,14 tells us, *"Like as a father pitieth his children, so the Lord pitieth them that fear him. For he knoweth our frame; he remembereth that we are dust."*

CHAPTER 13

THE BEAST RISES UP

Verses 1,2:

1. *And I stood upon the sand of the sea, and saw a beast rise up out of the sea, having seven heads and ten horns, and upon his horns ten crowns, and upon his heads the name of blasphemy.*

2. *And the beast which I saw was like unto a leopard, and his feet were as the feet of a bear, and his mouth as the mouth of a lion; and the dragon gave him his power, and his seat, and great authority.*

We see here the resurrected body of the anti-Christ, this beast, rises up *"out of the sea"*. In Revelation 11:7 and again in 17:8, it says that this beast *"ascendeth out of the bottomless pit"*. We know the Bible does not contradict itself, so it must be this *"sea"* and the *"bottomless pit"* are synonymous terms.

As we look, we see this beast had *"seven heads and ten horns"*. Upon these seven heads were written *"the name of blasphemy."* The original Greek text uses the word 'names' indicating there were different names for the various heads of this beast.

1. BLASPHEMY – This word and its derivatives is used 59 times in the Word of God. In the New Testament, it comes from the Greek word 'blasphemeo' meaning 'to speak evil against; to revile; to defame'.[1] Certainly, this is what the anti-Christ who is the beast came to do against the Most High God and His Christ.

---

[1] (Strong's #987)

2. AFFLICTION – The purpose of the enemy has always been to bring affliction to the children of God. Psalm 34:19 says, *"Many are the <u>afflictions</u> of the righteous; but the Lord delivereth him out of them all."* One of the first great afflictions we see in God's Word is when the Children of Israel were *"afflicted"* four hundred years while in the bondage of Egypt.

3. REBELLION – This was in the nature of this beast because he rebelled against the God of Heaven way back in the first place and was cast out to the earth. He is clearly called in Scripture *"the god of this world"*. (2 Cor. 4:4).

4. DECEIT – The trick of the enemy has always been to deceive God's people. The Word of God says, *"For there shall arise false Christs, and false prophets, and shall shew great signs and wonders; insomuch that, if it were possible, they shall <u>deceive</u> the very elect."* (Matt. 24:24). *"For many <u>deceivers</u> are entered into the world, who confess not that Jesus Christ is come in the flesh. This is a <u>deceiver</u> and an <u>antichrist.</u>"* (2 John 7).

5. IGNORANCE – The trick of religions down through the ages was to keep the people *ignorant* of the truth. In one of our early pastorates up in the north of the U.S., a precious German lady came into the meetings and accepted the Lord Jesus as her personal Savior. She continued to go to the religious church where she had been born and raised as she was the one who cleaned the church every week. The huge pulpit Bible lay open on the lectern and it happened to be at Acts 2:38. She read these words about *"repent and be baptized"* and went to ask the pastor what it meant. He scolded her and said it was not for her to read that Bible or to seek anything more than what he taught her.

The following week the Bible was again open to another passage about water baptism. Finally, she came to my husband and asked what this all meant. When she saw the truth, she insisted on being baptized by immersion. It was November in

Wisconsin, but the thought of the icy waters did not seem to bother Rosa. She had found the truth and she was going to walk in it.

"Ye shall know the truth, and the truth shall make you free!" (John 8:32).

6. ENCHANTMENT – There is probably nothing more enchanting than some religious ritual in some fabulous edifice called a church. With all of its pomp and ceremony, the crowds are almost hypnotized as they watch all of the goings-on. We visited the City of Rome not too long ago and saw all of the goings-on. There were thousands standing in the downpour of rain just waiting to get a fleeting glimpse of the pope. He came out for a brief moment, raised up two fingers to bless the people and returned from the balcony. The crowds thought they had gone to heaven. Later, in the Vatican bookstore, my husband asked one of the Papal Guards why the pope raised two fingers together. The young man spoke good English and jokingly said, "His Holiness was using super glue last night and got it stuck on his fingers." Seriously, though, we had a most unusual experience there in the center of *enchantment.*

I went to use the restroom and, while waiting, my husband found a quiet little nook and sat down to rest. There on a small table was a little card written in English. It said, "Guided tours for the devout every Wednesday at 3:00." He asked the guard how to get into one of these tours and was asked, "Are you devout?" Bob replied, "Oh, very devout to the Lord Jesus!" All we needed to do was to be there just a little before three on Wednesday afternoon. So there we were. About 38 people showed up as hardly anyone saw that little sign in the corner nook. It was only for the devout, after all.

A pretty, youthful looking Sister soon appeared clothed in a lovely light blue habit. She had long golden hair and spoke perfect English. While waiting I asked her where she was from. "Michigan" was her reply. We found out she was from Alma, Michigan and that is where I preached at the Women's Aglow meeting when the local Catholic priest was 'slain in the Spirit' and received the Baptism in the Spirit. What a small world! But this was not the real blessing. We went into secret places in the Vatican and were told so many unusual and interesting things.

At the close of the guided tour, a man and his wife spoke to our guide and asked this question. "Why in all this tour did you not mention a thing about the Blessed Mother?" Her answer astounded us. "Because this place is not dedicated to her. It is dedicated to her Son and our Only Savior, the Lord Jesus Christ!" We had been guided through the 'Enchanted Castle' by a secret agent of the Lord who was there to witness to the truth about Jesus.

7. DEATH – Spiritual ignorance, deceit and rebellion will ultimately bring on spiritual death. The purpose of the enemy is this very thing. Jesus taught us in John 10:10, *"The thief (the devil) cometh not, but for to steal, and to kill, and to destroy."*

As we look further at this beast, we see he bore the same nature as the various beasts that were revealed to the Prophet Daniel. First, it says that he was *"like a LEOPARD"*. When the anti-Christ appears on the earth, his conquest will be with swiftness, even as that of a leopard pouncing and springing suddenly upon his prey.

Next, we see *"his feet were as the feet of a BEAR"*. The bear has brute force and his feet are his strongest weapon. So will it be with the 'man of sin' who will be revealed in that day. Finally, we see *"his mouth was as the mouth of a LION"*. The lion's teeth and his mouth are his most powerful weapon so that he may devour his prey.

"Your adversary the devil, as a roaring <u>lion</u>, *walketh about, seeking whom he may devour. Whom resist stedfast in the faith …"* (1 Pet. 5:8,9

Verses 3-10:

3. *And I saw one of his heads as it were wounded to death; and his deadly wound was healed; and all the world wondered after the beast.*

4. *And they worshipped the dragon which gave power unto the beast; and they worshipped the beast, saying, Who is like unto the beast? Who is able to make war with him?*

5. *And there was given unto him a mouth speaking great things and blasphemies; and power was given unto him to continue forty and two months (3 ½ years)."*

6. *And he opened his mouth in blasphemy against God, to blaspheme his name, and his tabernacle, and them that dwell in heaven.*

7. *And it was given unto him to make war with the saints, and to overcome them; and power was given him over all kindreds, and tongues, and nations.*

8. *And all that dwell upon the earth shall worship him, whose names are not written in the book of life of the Lamb slain from the foundation of the world.*

9. *If any man have an ear, let him hear.*

10. *He that leadeth into captivity shall go into captivity; he that killeth with the sword must be killed with the sword. Here is the patience and the faith of the saints.*

Just as soon as the anti-Christ was revealed coming out of the bottomless pit, the sea, he received a "deadly wound". From II Thessalonians 2 verses 3 and 4, we know that something had to transpire to give him this deadly wound. *"Let no man deceive you by any means; for that day (of the rapture) shall not come, except there come a falling away first, and that* <u>man of sin</u> *be revealed, the* <u>son of perdition</u>; *Who opposeth and exalteth himself above all that is called God, or that is worshipped; so that he as God sitteth in the temple of God, shewing himself that he is God."*

Almost simultaneous to the revelation of the anti-Christ, comes the greatest event for overcomers that has or ever will transpire – 'The Rapture'. It is this amazing event that caused the *"deadly wound"* to the head of the anti-Christ. It was healed when so many that thought they were ready were not and were 'left behind'. This brought great glee to the archenemy of the Church and the deadly wound was healed. Far worse than a deadly wound was coming for this evil one as we shall see later on in Revelation.

This section of verses lets us know the first thing the anti-Christ does is to persecute those who are 'left behind'. God allows this persecution for a little season knowing His true saints, whose names were written in the Lamb's Book of Life, would not give in to the enemy nor take his mark or worship him. They knew better than this for they had been taught to never take the 'mark of the beast' no matter what.

Verses 11-13:

11. *And I beheld another beast coming up out of the earth; and he had two horns like a lamb, and he spake as a dragon.*

12. *And he exerciseth all the power of the first beast, whose deadly wound was healed.*

13. *And he doeth great wonders, so that he maketh fire come down from heaven on the earth in sight of men.*

Revelation 13 describes two of the greatest rebels of all history. One is the beast who came out of the sea and the second is *"another beast coming up out of the earth"*. The first beast, who came up out of the bottomless pit, the sea, was none other than the *anti-Christ* whose true identity we shall reveal shortly.

The second beast, who came out of the earth, was the *false prophet* who bore witness to the first beast. We see this clearly revealed if we look just a little ahead to Revelation 16:13, *"And I saw three unclean spirits like frogs come out of the mouth of the dragon (satan), and out of the mouth of the beast, and out of the mouth of the false prophet."*

Satan's trinity! Always the imitator of our Lord God! The false prophet is satan's imitation of the Holy Spirit. The Spirit of God did not come to speak of Himself, but to glorify the Lord Jesus Christ.

So here, we see this false prophet, not speaking of himself, but lifting up the anti-Christ. This false prophet *"had all the power of the first beast"* just like the Holy Spirit had all the power of the Lord Jesus. The Holy Spirit is called 'The Spirit of Truth'. Here we see 'the spirit of deceit'. Look at it with me.

Verses 14,15:

14. *And deceiveth them that dwell on the earth by the means of those miracles which he had power to do in the sight of the beast; saying to them that dwell on the earth, that they should make an image to the beast, which had the wound by a sword, and did live.*

15. *And he had power to give life unto the image of the beast, that the image of the beast should both speak, and cause that as many as would not worship the image of the beast should be killed.*

We must remember Lucifer is not omnipresent as is our great God. This is why he found it necessary to make images of this beast to send around the world that men might worship these images that had the power to speak. The Lord God Almighty distinctly forbids the worship of images. The anti-Christ promotes the worship of images.

"Thou shalt have no other gods before me. Thou shalt not make unto thee any graven image. Thou shalt not bow down thyself to them, nor serve them." (Exod. 20:2-5).

The worship of our wonderful Lord should be in the *"beauty of holiness"* and in the simplicity of the Spirit. The anti-Christ is bent on worship that is wrapped up in the trappings of everything but Jesus.

THE MARK OF THE BEAST

Verses 16-18:

16. *And he (the anti-Christ) causeth all, both small and great, rich and poor, free and bond, to receive a <u>mark</u> in their right hand, or in their foreheads;*

17. *And that no man might buy or sell, save he that had the <u>mark</u>, or the name of the beast, or the number of his name.*

18. *Here is wisdom. Let him that hath understanding count the number of the beast; for it is the number of a man; and his number is Six hundred three-score and six.* (Emphasis added.)

Three things are spoken of here concerning the Great Tribulation and those whose doom will be forever sealed by taking one or all of three things.

1. *The Mark of the Beast* - This identifying mark will be given in the right hand or the forehead with which the bearer will be able to buy and sell during this dreadful time upon the earth. With today's modern techniques this would be totally and easily possible to be done.

2. *The Name of the Beast* – Just as we as Christians bear the name of our Lord Jesus, so will those in the tribulation who pay homage to the beast bear his name. As sweet as is the name of Jesus, the name of the beast will be just as bitter.

3. *The Number of the Beast* – That infamous number is '666'. Much has been speculated as to the real meaning of this number. Some have said this is the number in the mitre or crown of the pope of Rome, but this idea is all too obvious. We will learn now who the anti-Christ really is and it will

certainly not be the pope even though he is falsely called and revered as the 'vicar' of Christ. I believe that '666' is simply a fullness, three, of the number of man which is six, again faking the Triune God.

WHO IS THE ANTI-CHRIST?

For a number of years I have pondered on this thought, "Who is the anti-Christ?" As we all know, any despotic ruler who ever came along was thought by some to be the anti-Christ. From Diocletian, the cruel Roman Emperor, to Pope Leo X, to Mussolini and Adolf Hitler, all have been suspects to be the 'man of sin'. None of these, of course, was that one who was to rule the world for a short space of 3 ½ years.

He, this 'man of sin', was to be far more than any of these could ever have been. He would not only have earthly powers behind him, he would have all the forces of the underworld at his disposal. Thank the Lord that God puts a short leash on him so that in all of the anti-Christ's devilish ways, he still can only go so far. When Almighty God says, "Enough is enough!" He really means it!

One day, while perusing a Christian bookstore, we came across a book on Revelation, written in the earlier part of the Twentieth Century, by Dr. Martin R. De Haan. He had been a medical doctor called to preach the gospel. He was pastor at Calvary Reformed Church in Grand Rapids, Michigan when he began to research the Book of Revelation. To his amazement, he found that there would be a 'catching away' of believers, a Tribulation period, and a thousand year reign of Christ upon the earth. This was against the a-millennial teaching of the Reformed Church so he left and founded Calvary Undenominational Church. His book, "The Chemistry of the Blood" is still being sold in Christian bookstores to this day.

In his study of the Scriptures, Dr. De Haan discovered an amazing fact of the striking similarity in God's Word between two personages. One was Judas Iscariot, the betrayer of our Lord Jesus. The other was the anti-Christ himself. He found what was said of the one, was also said of the other. Look with me at what the Bible says about these two beings.

1. *"the son of perdition"*

This phrase is found only twice in the entire Bible. The first instance applies to Judas Iscariot; the second to the beast who is the anti-Christ.

Jesus words concerning Judas Iscariot, *"Those that thou gavest me I have kept, and none of them is lost, but the son of perdition; that the Scripture might be fulfilled."* (John 17:12).

Paul's writing concerning the anti-Christ, *"Let no man deceive you by any means; for that day shall not come, except there come a falling away first, and that man of sin be revealed, the son of perdition."* (2 Thess. 2:3).

2. *"one of you IS a devil"*

These are strong words spoken by our Lord Jesus about Judas Iscariot. Jesus did not say that he was demon-possessed or that Judas just had a devil. The Greek word used here is 'diabolos'[2] and refers directly to satan or the devil. No mistaking here what Jesus said about Judas.

"Have I not chosen you twelve, and one of you IS A DEVIL! He spake of Judas Iscariot the son of Simon; for it was he that should betray him, being one of the twelve." (John 6:70,71).

This same word 'diabolos' is used for satan, the devil, who empowers the beast who is the anti-Christ. It appears from this that Judas Iscariot and the anti-Christ beast are

---

[2] (Strong's #1228)

one and the same or, at least, possess the same demonic spirit.

3. *"to his own place"*

These words are used of Judas Iscariot following his betrayal of Jesus and his suicide of remorse. *"This ministry and apostleship from which Judas by transgression fell that he might go <u>to his own place (the bottomless pit).</u>"* (Acts 1:25).

Compare this to what it says in Revelation 17:8, *"The beast (anti-Christ) that thou sawest <u>was, and is not;</u> and shall <u>ascend out of the bottomless pit, and go into perdition.</u>"*

Judas Iscariot was called by Jesus *"the son of perdition"* (note the word *"perdition"* used here in this text), '<u>WAS</u>' on the earth as one of the disciples.   '<u>IS NOT</u>' as he died and went *"to his own place"*.   '<u>SHALL ASCEND</u>' out of *"the bottomless pit (his own place)"*.

4. *"the betrayer"*

The Greek word for 'betray' is 'paradidomi'[3], which means 'to betray, to deliver up, to put in bondage, to hinder, a traitor'. *"Jesus said, Verily I say unto you, One of you which eateth with me <u>shall betray me.</u>"* (Mark 14:18, emphasis added). *"Judas Iscariot, which also was <u>the traitor.</u>"* (Luke 6:16, emphasis added). *"And Judas also, <u>which betrayed him.</u>"* (John 18:2).

There is no question Judas Iscariot was all of these things, but what about the anti-Christ? Who could be more of *"a betrayer"* than him? His betrayal began all the way back in eternity when, as Lucifer, he betrayed the Lord God and was cast out of heaven. Ever since then he has done nothing but betray. He betrayed the first man and woman

---

[3] (Strong's #3860)

when he said in the Garden of Eden, *"And the serpent (satan) said unto the woman, Ye shall not surely die."* (Gen. 3:4).

His lies and betrayal have continued ever since. Jesus said of the enemy, the devil, these words, *"he was a murderer from the beginning, and abode not in the truth, because there is no truth in him. When he speaketh a lie, he speaketh of his own; for he is a liar, and the father of it."* (John 8:44).

I studied for many hours and searched out many Scriptures to find out if the Word of God really told us who the anti-Christ was. It became very clear to me that Judas Iscariot fits the bill for this position. I taught this and, while some raised their eyebrows, others accepted it much to their own amazement. Most readers of God's Word have never put it all together. You make your own decision having now read all that I have written concerning the subject, "Who is the anti-Christ?"

Whatever you choose to believe, just don't plan to be here during his short reign upon the earth!

CHAPTER 14

144,000 REDEEMED IN HEAVEN

Verses 1-5:

1. *And I looked, and, lo, a Lamb stood on the mount Sion, and with him an hundred forty and four thousand, having his Father's name written in their foreheads.*

2. *And I heard a voice from heaven, as the voice of many waters, and as the voice of a great thunder; and I heard the voice of harpers harping with their harps;*

3. *And they sung as it were a new song before the throne, and before the four beasts (living creatures), and the elders; and no man could learn that song but the hundred and forty and four thousand, which were redeemed from the earth.*

4. *These are they which were not defiled with women; for they are virgins. These are they which follow the Lamb whithersoever he goeth. These were redeemed from among men being the firstfruits unto God and to the Lamb.*

5. *And in their mouth was found no guile; for they are without fault before the throne of God.*

This is not the same group recorded in Chapter 7.

Revelation 7	Revelation 14
On the earth (vs. 1,3)	In heaven (vs. 1,3)
Jews from tribes (vs. 4)	Redeemed from earth (vs. 3)
Protected by God (vs. 3)	Worshipping God (vs. 3)
Seal in foreheads (vs. 3)	Name in foreheads (vs. 1)

More is said in these verses about this special group of 144,000 as to their identity in the Kingdom of God.

1. With the Lamb on Heavenly Mount Zion.
2. The Father's Name written IN their foreheads.
3. Singing a 'new song' before the throne of God.
4. Not defiled with women.
5. Follow the Lamb withersoever He goes.
6. Redeemed from among men.
7. Firstfruits company unto God and the Lamb.
8. No guile in their mouth.
9. Without fault before the throne of God.

We have already been introduced to a group of this number – 144,000 – in Chapter 7. They are literal Jews, the remnant that God promised to Abraham. This group of Jews is preserved throughout the Great Tribulation. They are on the literal earth during this time.

We know that there is an earthly Mount Zion in Jerusalem, but there is also a heavenly Mount Zion as spoken of Hebrews 12:22, *"But ye are come unto Mount Zion, and unto the city of the Living God, the heavenly Jerusalem, and unto an innumerable company of angels ..."*

Here in the heavenlies we find this second group of 144,000 who have attained unto the highest order of believers. These are they *"who follow the Lamb whithersoever He goeth"*. They love Him so much they will not leave His side. They sing the special song that they alone can sing. Their voices were like the sound of many waters. They were without fault or guile.

The church is spoken of in the female gender. These following the Lamb were not defiled with church rules and man-made doctrines. They were pure virgins and desired only the pure truth of the Word of God. They followed Jesus with no holding back. The church is very important as we have seen in Chapter 12, however, many churches in these last days refuse to allow God's Holy Spirit to move or do any of His marvelous works in their midst. As Jesus said, *"Ye have made the Word of God of none effect by your vain traditions!"* (Mark 7:13).

I believe that this company of 144,000 is a 'first-fruits' company taken out from the church who have attained the highest realm with Jesus as the "select of the elect".

"Till we all come in the unity of the faith, and of the knowledge of the Son of God, unto a perfect (fully mature) man, unto the measure of the stature of the fullness of Christ ...That we may grow up into Him in all things, which is the head, even Christ." (Eph. 4:13,15).

"Of His own will begat He us with the word of truth, that we should be a kind of firstfruits of His creatures." (James 1:18).

So many are bound by religion and cannot be free in the Lord. Others have never grown up in Christ, but have stayed at one level in their Christian lives. Open up to Jesus and follow Him as He leads you to deeper depths and higher heights.

In Chapter 7, the 144,000 literal Jews were sealed in their foreheads as *"the servants of our God"*. The seal that the 144,000 in this chapter wear is *'the seal of the Bride'*.

In Verse 3 of this chapter we see that the Bride is singing *"a new song before the throne, and before the four beasts (living creatures), and the elders; and no man could learn that song but the hundred and forty and four thousand, which were redeemed from the earth!"* Even those wonderful living creatures and the elders around the throne could not sing this song, only the Bride of the Lamb was given this glorious song.

THE ANGELS OF HEAVEN

Verses 6-11:

6. *And I saw another angel fly in the midst of heaven, having the everlasting gospel to preach unto them that dwell on the earth, and to every nation, and kindred, and tongue, and people.*

7. *Saying with a loud voice, Fear God, and give glory to him; for the hour of his judgment is come, and worship him that made heaven, and earth, and the sea, and the fountains of waters.*

8. *And there followed another angel, saying, Babylon is fallen, is fallen, that great city, because she made all nations drink of the wine of the wrath of her fornication.*

9. *And the third angel followed them, saying with a loud voice, If any man worship the beast and his image, and receive his mark in his forehead, or in his hand,*

10. *The same shall drink of the wine of the wrath of God, which is poured out without mixture into the cup of his indignation; and he shall be tormented with fire and brimstone in the presence of the holy angels, and in the presence of the Lamb;*

11. *And the smoke of their torment ascendeth up forever and ever; and they have no rest day nor night, who worship the beast and his image, and whosoever receiveth the mark of his name.*

Earlier in the writings of this book, I listed all of the "Angels of the Apocalypse". In this chapter there are more angels revealed than in any other. In Verse 6, we find the first of these many angels, herein called by John *"another angel"*. This amazing angel flew in the midst of heaven *"having the everlasting gospel to preach unto them that dwell on the earth, and to every nation, and kindred, and tongue, and people."*

God gave "The Great Commission" to His followers to bring the gospel to "all the world". In our text here the day of grace has come to a close and a 'special angel' is given the task to wind up the era called 'time'. Oh, how great are the mercies of our God that even those who would not listen to the church and the preachers in the Day of Grace would still have opportunity to hear *"the everlasting gospel"* via a special angel of grace.

In Verse 8 following this angel of grace came *"another angel"* declaring *"Babylon is fallen, is fallen, that great city, because she made all nations drink of the wine of the wrath of her fornication (uncleanness)."* We are going to see shortly just which city on earth is what the Bible calls *"that great city"*. This term is mentioned many times in the Book of Revelation, as we shall see.

Now, we see yet again in Verse 9 *"the third angel"*. This angel warns against the worship of the "beast", which is the anti-Christ, and the terrible results of such worship and allegiance to satan, the beast, the evil one.

Finally, in this passage in Verse 10 it speaks of *"the holy angels"* as a company of angelic beings before the throne of God and of the Lamb.

Verses 12, 13:

12. *Here is the patience of the saints; here are they that keep the commandments of God, and the faith of Jesus.*

13. *And I heard a voice from heaven saying unto me, Write, Blessed are the dead which die in the Lord from henceforth; Yea, saith the Spirit, that they may rest from their labours; and their works do follow them.*

The recommendation of our Lord comes to those who in the time of trial and test follow the Lamb all the way. Here our Lord reveals the attributes of His true followers.

1. *"The patience of the saints"*

One of the marks of the overcoming saints of the ages is that they had long-patience during their sojourn on this earth. In this rushing day in which we live, it is really difficult for us to have such patience as we are living in the days of "instant everything".

2. *"Keep the commandments of God"*

We have been given the Golden Rule, the Ten Commandments as our rule of faith and conduct. The true followers of the Lamb will keep His Word and His Commandments.

3. *"The faith of Jesus"*

Jesus taught us concerning *"mustard seed faith"* and let us know that it could move mountains. Oh, that we could have this kind of faith in this our day.

Verse 13 has been used as a funeral sermon by my husband as well as countless numbers of preachers. Even though it really refers to the end-times, yet the Word of God is applicable to all eras of time. It is so assuring to know that those who have served the Lord throughout their lives are now *"resting from their labours"*, and the works that they have done for Christ on earth, are still remembered even after they have gone on – *"And their works do follow them."*

THE SON OF MAN ON A WHITE CLOUD

Verses 14-20:

14. *And I looked, and behold a white cloud, and upon the cloud one sat like unto the Son of Man, having on his head a golden crown, and in his hand a sharp sickle.*

15. *And another angel came out of the temple, crying with a loud voice to him that sat on the cloud, Thrust in thy sickle, and reap; for the time is come for thee to reap; for the harvest of the earth is ripe.*

16. *And he that sat on the cloud thrust in his sickle on the earth; and the earth was reaped.*

17. *And another came out of the temple which is in heaven, he also having a sharp sickle.*

18. *And another angel came out from the altar, which had power over fire; and cried with a loud cry to him that had the sharp sickle, saying, Thrust in thy sharp sickle, and gather the clusters of the vine of the earth, for her grapes are fully ripe.*

19. *And the angel thrust in his sickle into the earth, and gathered the vine of the earth, and cast it into the great winepress of the wrath of God.*

20. *And the winepress was trodden without the city, and blood came out of the winepress, even unto the horse bridles by the space of a thousand and six hundred furlongs.*

We now see the final angels of this chapter revealed in these verses. Most importantly, however, is *"One like unto the Son of Man"*. He was the same One that old King Nebuchadnezzar saw in the fiery furnace when he declared, *"Did we not cast three men bound into the midst of the fire? They answered and said unto the king, True, O king. He answered and said, Lo, I see four men loose, walking in the midst of the fire, and they have no hurt; and the form of the fourth is like the Son of God!"* (Dan.3:24,25).

He was the same one that Isaiah the Prophet saw when he said in Isaiah 9:6, *"For unto us a child is born, unto us a Son is given; and the government shall be upon His shoulder; and His name shall be called Wonderful, Counsellor, The Mighty God, The Everlasting Father, The Prince of Peace!"*

Now John sees Him in the Patmos vision as the same Eternal God, One with the Father through all eternity.

Let's go back to the angels of Revelation 14. *"Another angel came out of the temple"*. This angel declares to the Lord sitting upon the white cloud *"The harvest of the earth is ripe!"* We have been to over sixty nations of the world in our missionary ministry and we can truly say with this end time angel – *"The harvest of the earth is ripe!"*

Never has there been a time in history when more people in more nations are being touched with this glorious gospel than right now in this 21st Century. Through great crusades, through national pastors, by means of radio and television and by dedicated missionaries, the nations are being touched with the gospel of our Lord Jesus Christ.

"And this gospel of the kingdom shall be preached in all the world for a witness unto all nations; and then shall the end come!" (Matt. 24:14).

This is the mandate of the church and it is happening!

Next, comes an angel out of the temple of heaven who also has a sharp sickle, and then another angel from out of the altar which had power over fire. This great angel reaped in the vines of the earth and cast them into the winepress of Almighty God. With this the blood flowed even unto the bridles of the horses. This is upon the earth during the Great Tribulation.

CHAPTER 15

SONG OF MOSES & THE LAMB

Verses 1-4:

1. And I saw another sign in heaven, great and marvelous, seven angels having the seven last plagues; for in them is filled up the wrath of God.

2. And I saw as it were a sea of glass mingled with fire; and them that had gotten the victory over the beast, and over his image, and over his mark, and over the number of his name, stand on the sea of glass, having the harps of God.

3. And they sang <u>the song of Moses the servant of God, and the song of the Lamb</u>, saying, Great and marvelous are thy works, Lord God Almighty; just and true are thy ways, thou King of saints.

4. Who shall not fear thee, O Lord, and glorify thy name? for thou only art holy; for all nations shall come and worship before thee; for thy judgments are made manifest.

Revelation 15 is a continuation of the previous chapter and its brief eight verses present a picture of the redeemed that have not worshipped the beast and have escaped the judgments of Almighty God.

The first verse of this chapter refers to the seven angels carrying the seven last plagues of the wrath of God upon unrepentant humanity. These are described in detail in Chapter 16 of Revelation. These plagues are poured out at the very end of the 3½ years of Great Tribulation known as the outpouring of 'The Wrath of God'. This is not the terror of the anti-Christ; this is the wrath of Almighty God.

While these groups of believers shown us in verses 2 to 4 are on the *'sea of glass mingled with fire'*, it seems quite apparent that they are somehow taken up to this place in heaven prior to the outpouring of God's wrath. They may have missed the original "catching away", but because they overcame the anti-Christ by refusing to bow down to him, they now have escaped the final terrible days of Tribulation.

We note here that they overcame in these four distinct categories:

1 – Over the beast himself.
2 – Over his image that was made to speak.
3 – Over his mark which we know to be 666.
4 - Over his name which denotes his satanic nature.

This took a lot of overcoming, but the results are proven to be worth it all as they now are on the *"sea of glass"* and singing the songs of the redeemed, *"the song of Moses and the Lamb"*. Even though the trials of life sometimes seem to be more than we can bear, think of the blessed time that will ours, as overcomers, when we stand in that eternal day in the setting that is described here.

In Chapter 4, we see this same *"sea of glass"*, but now in this scene it is a *"sea of glass mingled with fire"*. The redeemed standing here on this glassy sea had gone through the fires of Tribulation and had gotten the victory as Revelation 12 says, *"By the blood of the Lamb and the word of their testimony!"*

"All nations shall come and worship before thee!" Today, there are many nations in this world that are totally atheistic and others that are totally Islamic or bound by other religions. We have found that even in these nations God has His own elect who are worshipping Him in secret.

The day will be coming when Paul's words in Philippians 2:9-11 will totally come to pass, *"Wherefore God also hath highly exalted him, and given him a name which is above every name; That at the name of Jesus <u>every knee should bow</u> of things in heaven, and things in earth, and things under the earth; And that <u>every tongue should confess</u> that Jesus Christ is Lord, to the glory of God the Father."*

In that day the so-called secret believers will no longer have to keep secret, as they will openly worship the Lord along with all the nations of the earth. We have watched in heathen nations as simple devout people have worshipped the only gods they know, those made out of wood or stone. This is why we have the Great Commission of our Lord Jesus, that we may point them to the one true and living God.

Years ago, we came across a missionary song that so touched our hearts that we began to use it in our missions meetings. Kenneth Robison, an Assemblies of God missionary to India wrote it. It so expresses exactly what the heathen in the nations are doing to try to reach God.

Let the words touch your heart as they did ours.

> I saw him in the dust bending low,
> 'Neath the curse of his dark pagan woe;
> He worshipped gods of stone and of gold,
> For of Christ He had never been told.
>
> I watched him in the hot afternoon,
> As he knelt in a shrine full of gloom;
> His idols having eyes could not see,
> They had ears but could not hear his plea.
>
> The rivers where he bathed day by day,
> Failed to cleanse his deep error away;
> I watched him as he rolled in the dust

For he knew not the Christ whom we trust.

A leper deeply stained with his blight,
Hung'ring soul, filled with want needing sight
An outcast, seized by torment and shame,
He found none who could cure his deep pain.

Chorus:
Then I whispered that sweet name of Jesus,
And a light broke across his dark face,
There in the night he found Jesus
And bathed in the fount of God's grace!

THE TEMPLE OF THE TABERNACLE

Verses 5-8:

5. *And after that I looked, and, behold, the temple of the tabernacle of the testimony in heaven was opened;*

6. *And the seven angels came out of the temple, having the seven plagues, clothed in pure and white linen, and having their breasts girded with golden girdles.*

7. *And one of the four beasts (living creatures) gave unto the seven angels seven golden vials full of the wrath of God, who liveth forever and ever.*

8. *And the temple was filled with smoke from the glory of God, and from his power; and no man was able to enter into the temple, till the seven plagues of the seven angels were fulfilled.*

The age in which we now live is called in Scripture, *"the dispensation of the grace of God"* (Eph. 3:2). It began with the first coming of Christ and will end with the second coming of Christ. The same Apostle, who is writing this Revelation of Jesus Christ, writes to us in his gospel these words, *"For the law was given by Moses, but grace and truth came by Jesus Christ!"* (John 1:17).

Following this 2,000+ year period, will be the events portrayed here in Revelation. Even though these two chapters (15 & 16) tell us of the wrath of God being outpoured upon unrepentant humanity, the very vials of this wrath come out of His Holiness from the most holy place of *"the temple of the tabernacle in heaven"*. The angels who come out with the plagues from that most holy place are clothed in pure white linen to represent the eternal holiness of the Lord God.

Only three times in the entire Word of God do we find anyone clothed in *'White Linen'*. The first incident is that of the worshippers in the Tabernacle of David. It says in II Chronicles 5:12, *"And the Levites which were the singers...being arrayed in <u>white linen</u>...were as one to make one sound to be heard in praising and thanking the Lord...then the house was filled with a cloud...for the glory of the Lord had filled the house of God."*

The second place where the clothing of *"white linen"* is mentioned is here in our text concerning the angels of *"the temple of the tabernacle in heaven...clothed in pure and <u>white linen</u>."*

Finally, in the last part of Book of Revelation, we see the Bride, the Lamb's wife, and here is her description. First, she is found as that army of heaven returning to the earth with Christ at His coming, *"And the armies which were in heaven followed him (Christ) upon white horses, clothed in <u>fine linen, white and clean</u>."* (Rev.19:14).

Then we find this same lovely bride at the Marriage Supper of the Lamb, *"Let us be glad and rejoice and give honour to him; for the marriage of the Lamb is come, and his wife hath made herself ready. And to her was granted that she should be arrayed in fine <u>linen, clean and white</u>: for the fine linen is the righteousness of saints. And he saith unto me, Write, Blessed are they which are called unto the marriage supper of the Lamb!"* (Rev.19:7-9).

The same glory that came into the Tabernacle of David in the Old Testament so that the priests could not stand, is this glory that we now see in *"the temple of the tabernacle in heaven"*. It says, *"the temple was filled with smoke from the glory of God!"* He is the Lord who changes not. If His glory was manifest in David's day of old, of course it will be the same glory in eternity.

Many times throughout the years of our pastoring, the glory cloud of the Lord has come down in our meetings. Sometimes in was like a literal cloud that you could see, but most often it was a sense of a weight of glory that just rested upon the congregation as God let His presence be known. The Hebrew word for *"glory"* is *'kabod'*[1] and literally means 'weight', but in the sense of a 'weight of splendor'. In the New Testament, the word *'glory'* comes from the Greek word *'doxa'*[2] meaning 'glory, worship, praise'. This is where we get the name of the hymn of praise called the *"Doxology"*.

> Praise God from whom all blessings flow.
> Praise Him all creatures here below.
> Praise Him above, ye heavenly hosts.
> Praise Father, Son and Holy Ghost. Amen.

Now the Eternal God of love and mercy does something that seems so contrary to His nature, He pours out His wrath upon unrepentant humanity. He does not pour it out so much because of their sin as much as the fact that they failed to repent or call upon Him even when they could. Sin was judged at Calvary, but men failed to accept that judgment so now must face the wrath of an angry God. Revelation 16:11 tells us that after these plagues when men should have called on God for mercy, instead they did this, *"And they blasphemed the God of heaven because of their pains and their sores, and repented not of their deeds!"* *"It is a fearful thing to fall into the hands of the living God!"* (Heb. 10:31).

---

[1] (Strong's #3519)
[2] (Strong's #1391)

CHAPTER 16

THE VIALS OF GOD'S WRATH

Verse 1:

And I heard a great voice out of the temple saying to the seven angels, Go your ways, and pour out the vials of the wrath of God upon the earth.

With the pouring out of the seven vials of the seven plagues upon the earth, will come the end of the period of God's righteous judgments upon the rebellious earth. The pouring out of the last vial will signal the return of Christ to the earth with His white-horse army.

"And I saw heaven opened, and behold a white horse; and he that sat upon him was called Faithful and True, and in righteousness he doth judge and make war...and the armies which were in heaven followed him upon white horses clothed in fine linen, white and clean." (Rev.19:11,14).

A true and righteous earthly father would never deliberately hurt or plague his children anymore than a truly righteous God would pour out His wrath upon His own children.

No, this brief period of time during which God pours out His wrath, will be only upon the unrighteous who refused to hear His voice or to repent of their wicked deeds.

This is the wrath of God poured out at the very end of the Great Tribulation period.

Verses 2-12:

2. *And the first (angel) went, and poured out his vial upon the earth; and there fell a noisome and grievous sore upon the men which had the mark of the beast, and upon them which worshipped his image.*

3. *And the second angel poured out his vial upon the sea; and it became as the blood of a dead man; and every living soul died in the sea.*

4. *And the third angel poured out his vial upon the rivers and the fountains of waters; and they became blood.*

5. *And I heard the angel of the waters say, Thou art righteous, O Lord, which art, and wast, and shalt be, because thou hast judged thus.*

6. *For they have shed the blood of saints and prophets, and thou hast given them blood to drink; for they are worthy.*

7. *And I heard another out of the altar say, Even so , Lord God Almighty, true and righteous are thy judgments.*

8. *And the fourth angel poured out his vial upon the sun; and power was given unto him to scorch men with fire.*

9. *And men were scorched with great heat, and blasphemed the name of God, which hath power over these plagues; and they repented not to give him glory.*

10. *And the fifth angel poured out his vial upon the seat of the beast; and his kingdom was full of darkness; and they gnawed their tongues for pain.*

11. *And blasphemed the God of heaven because of their pains and their sores, and repented not of their deeds.*

12. *And the sixth angel poured out his vial upon the great river Euphrates; and the water thereof was dried up, that the way of the kings of the east might be prepared.*

During the 3 ½ years, after the true church has been caught away, the earth will be plagued by war, pestilence, destruction and death under the cruel hand of the 'Man of Sin", the anti-Christ. Nearly half of the entire population of the earth will perish during this brief period. God's word says there has never been a period like it and there will never be another after it. *"For then shall be great tribulation, such as was not since the beginning of the world to this time, no, nor ever shall be."* (Matt. 24:21).

We are so grateful that God has provided a way of escape through our Lord Jesus Christ if we will only trust Him and walk closely to Him in the days of our life upon this earth. We came from eternity and are going back to eternity, but let's make the best of our lives while we are here on this earth.

THE END IS NEAR

With the pouring out of the vials of God's wrath as we have just read here in this text, comes the end of the judgment of God upon the rebellion of humankind. The next judgment of God upon all humanity is at the 'Great White Throne' found in Revelation 20.

Notice with me that the plagues which follow the outpouring of the vials of God's wrath have a striking similarity to the awful plagues which fell upon Egypt during the days of Moses and the deliverance of God's people in that day. When Pharaoh persecuted the children of Israel in Egypt and refused to let them go to the land of promise, God sent plagues upon them until Pharaoh and his house had been destroyed. That judgment of plagues was a foreshadow of these plagues we now study. The plagues of Pharaoh's day were limited to the land of Egypt; those described here will fall on the whole earth.

We see in this study that the various plagues were poured out on different places, the first on the land, the next on the sea, then on the rivers and then on the sun. The fifth one was poured out on the very seat of the beast, who is the anti-Christ, and the next upon the great Euphrates River which runs through the very heart of Babylon which is today the City of Baghdad in Iraq. The final one was poured into the very air that men breathe.

One little phrase in Verse 9 shows us the justice of all this, *"God which hath power over these plagues"*. If we believe that God made the sun, we can believe that He can darken the sun or increase its power and heat. If we, likewise, believe that God made the waters, we can believe that He can turn them into blood at His own will.

WHAT ABOUT TODAY'S BABYLON?

Much contention has taken place since the invasion by the U.S. of the Nation of Iraq, the Babylon of today. Was it a justifiable war? Should we have become involved in the affairs of the Islamic world? Did Saddam Hussein truly have weapons of mass destruction? Who can honestly answer all of these questions? This we do know about 'Today's Babylon':

Saddam Hussein, the self-appointed dictator of Iraq, declared himself to be the 'incarnation' of the old King Nebuchadnezzar. As such, he proceeded to rebuild, at an enormous cost, the original 'Hanging Gardens of Babylon', one of the seven wonders of the ancient world. He had visions of grandeur similar to those of most dictators down through history. Huge statues of himself dotted the landscape of Baghdad and the nation. The U.S. Armed Forces now utilize the extravagant palaces that dot the landscape of the city. Perhaps he was, at least in his own mind, the return of Nebuchadnezzar. If so, a true 'Daniel' was really needed to show the way of escape from all of the trouble that has happened because of this one man.

Iraq was the site of the *"Garden of Eden"*, God's original paradise for His glorious creation. How do we know this? Because Genesis 2:10 tells us this, *"A river went out of Eden to water the garden; and from thence it was parted, and became into four heads."*

This Scripture goes on to name those four rivers and among them are the *'River Euphrates'* and the *'Tigris River'*, called here 'Hiddekel'. One only need follow the news of all that is going on in Baghdad to know that these two rivers flow right through the midst of that city.

It was into Babylonian captivity that the Nation of Israel was taken back in the days of Daniel and the Hebrew children. So we see that today's Iraq plays an important place in the Biblical history of Israel.

Verses 13,14:

13. *And I saw three unclean spirits like frogs come out of the mouth of the dragon, and out of the mouth of the beast, and out of the mouth of the false prophet.*

14. *For they are the spirits of devils, working miracles, which go forth unto the kings of the earth and of the whole world, to gather them to the battle of that great day of God Almighty.*

SATAN'S TRINITY

Just as our God is a Triune God revealed to us in the Father, the Son and the Holy Spirit, so is the liar, the imitator of God like a trinity. Nowhere is it better revealed than right here in these two verses.

Satan's Trinity – 'The dragon, the beast, the false prophet'.

They appear as *'unclean spirits'* like frogs. "Why like frogs?" was the question I asked when reading this? They were not literal frogs, but *"like frogs"*, that is similar in appearance and character as frogs. Frogs like to live in darkness, in the swamps of mire along with the foul waters and the poisonous snakes. These unclean spirits represented by frogs are lovers of darkness and every unclean thing. Out of this darkness, they will bring forth their deceit with the working of lying miracles. As always, the enemy is counterfeiting the real thing with his deception. Frogs are only found in a few distinct places in Scripture. First, we see them in Exodus 8 in the plagues of Egypt. Then, the Psalmist rehearses the plagues and reports again about the frogs. Finally, here in our text when frogs are likened to *'unclean spirits'*.

Verses 15-21:

15. *Behold, I come as a thief. Blessed he that watcheth, and keepeth his garments, let he walk naked, and they see his shame.*

16. *And he gathered them together into a place called in the Hebrew tongue <u>Armageddon</u>.*

17. *And the seventh angel poured out his vial into the air; and there came a great voice out of the temple of heaven, from the throne, saying, IT IS DONE!*

18. *And there were voices, and thunders, and lightnings; and there was a great earthquake such as was not since men were upon the earth, so mighty and earthquake, and so great.*

19. *And <u>the great city</u> was divided into three parts, and the cities of the nations fell; and great Babylon came in remembrance before God, to give unto her the cup of the wine of the fierceness of his wrath.*

20. *And every island fled away, and the mountains were not found.*

21. *And there fell upon men a great hail out of heaven, every stone about the weight of a talent (130 pounds); and men blasphemed God because of the plague of the hail; for the plague thereof was exceeding great. (Emphasis added.)*

So ends the wrath of God that is to be poured out in the last months of the Great Tribulation upon unrepentant humanity. Instead of crying out to God for mercy, the Word says that they *"blasphemed God"*. This is recorded three times in the chapter. We need only look to the Book of Jude just prior to this Book of Revelation to see Jude's description of these *"brute beasts"* as he calls them. Jude speaks clearly of this 'day of judgment' that is coming in these words, *"...Behold, the Lord cometh with ten thousands of his saints, To execute judgment upon all (unrepentant mankind), and to convince all that are ungodly among them of their ungodly deeds which they have ungodly committed, and of all their hard speeches which ungodly sinners have spoken against him (the Lord)."* (Jude 14,15).

I COME AS A THIEF!

Here in Verse 15, the Lord Jesus speaks to John the Revelator to tell him, *"Behold, I come as a thief"*. The Apostle Paul also heard these words and recorded them in First Thessalonians 5:2,4, *"For yourselves know perfectly that the day of the Lord so cometh as a thief in the night. But ye, brethren, are not in darkness, that that day should overtake you as a thief."*

Peter wrote in Second Peter 3:10, *"But the day of the Lord will come as a thief in the night."*

As Verse 15 challenges each of us, we need to watch and pray and keep ourselves unspotted from this old world that we may be ready for that day of Christ's appearing.

Take special note of Verse 17 of this text, *"It is done!"*

Instantly upon reading this, my mind went to the words of our Lord Jesus as He hung upon the cross, *"IT IS FINISHED!"*— the very same words!

When Almighty God says something is done or finished you can take it to the bank. God means what He says! And when He finally says *"Enough is enough"* then look out because the hammer is about to fall. That day, beloved, is fast approaching. It is in the words of a little chorus we used to sing in our services:

> Jesus, getting us ready for that great day;
> Jesus, getting us ready for that great day.
> Jesus, getting us ready for that great day;
> Who shall be able to stand!

On Calvary Jesus finished and completed the eternal plan of salvation. Nothing more can be added to it even though religion has certainly tried to add many things down through the ages. Now, at the end of this age, God says, *"It is done!"* – *"Time shall be no more!"*

ARMAGEDDON

When the seventh vial is poured out, we will have reached the Battle of Armageddon. So much has been made of one verse in the Bible! Men have written books, motion pictures have been produced, sermons have been preached, challenges have been made. *Get ready for Armageddon!* Yet, this word only appears one time in all the Word of God. Just one time! So why so much commotion? The word simply describes the great battle between the forces of good and evil, but WOW what a battle it will be in that day.

We have visited many times on our trips to Israel the 'Valley of Megiddo' where the infamous Battle of Armageddon will supposedly be fought. It is a vast valley and it is certainly possible that it could and will actually happen in that exact place. Whatever happens we know that it is all in the hands of our God and of His Christ. The final word is simply this:

HE SHALL REIGN FOREVER AND EVER!

We see in this portion of this chapter once again this phrase *"the great city"* (verse 19). Twice before in our study we have seen this mentioned. The first time in Revelation 11:8

where it says, *"the great city...where also our Lord was crucified."* (Emphasis added.) Again in 14:8 it tells us, *"Babylon is fallen, is fallen, that great city"*.

Once again, in Chapter 17, we find reference to this amazing city. It is Chapter 18, however, where five references are made to this city. When we study Chapter 18, I will share with you my reasoning for what city on earth is *"that great city"*.

CHAPTER 17

MYSTERY BABYLON

Verses 1-5:

1. And there came one of the seven angels which had the seven vials, and talked with me, saying unto me, Come hither; I will shew unto thee the judgment of the great whore that sitteth upon many waters.

2. With whom the kings of the earth have committed fornication, and the inhabitants of the earth have been made drunk with the wine of her fornication.

3. So he carried me away in the spirit into the wilderness; and I saw a woman sit upon a scarlet coloured beast, full of names of blasphemy, having seven heads and ten horns.

4. And the woman was arrayed in purple and scarlet colour, and decked with gold and precious stones and pearls, having a golden cup in her hand full of abominations and filthiness of her fornication;

5. And upon her forehead was a name written, MYSTERY, BABYLON THE GREAT, THE MOTHER OF HARLOTS AND ABOMINATIONS OF THE EARTH!

We must now analyze what the Holy Spirit is showing John on Patmos concerning the *"great whore"* of the end times as recorded here in Revelation. We know that a whore, a harlot, a prostitute is an unclean woman given to adultery, fornication and sexual immorality.

In this case in our text this uncleanness refers to spiritual immorality rather than sexual.

First of all in Verse 1 we find the scarlet woman *"sitting upon many waters"* speaking of her worldwide influence over the *"waters"* which speak of humanity and the nations.

Next, we find in Verse 2 that she has so influenced the nations and its leaders as to make them drunk, as it were, with her beguilement and enticements.

In Verse 3, the Spirit shows John that this woman is riding on none other than the beast or the anti-Christ who has arisen up out of the sea of humanity who is full of blasphemy.

"And I saw a beast rise up out of the sea (of humanity) having seven heads and ten horns, and upon his horns ten crowns (kings/leaders), and upon his heads the name of blasphemy." (Rev. 13:1).

Verse 4, this woman decked in colors and with jewelry, but also having *"a golden cup in her hand"*. In the Old Testament, we see a prophetic word to confirm that which we see here in Revelation.

"Babylon (the woman) hath been a golden cup in the Lord's hand, that made all the earth drunken; the nations have drunken of her wine; therefore the nations are mad. Babylon is suddenly fallen and destroyed; howl for her; take balm for her pain, if so be she may be healed. We would have healed Babylon, but she is NOT healed; forsake her, and let us go everyone into his own country; for her judgment reacheth unto heaven, and is lifted up even to the skies." (Jer.51:7-10, emphasis added).

Oh, how the Lord had desired to use 'this Babylon', the fallen church. He even declares that she had been at one time *"a golden cup"* in His hand, but now look how she had fallen to the depths of spiritual fornication and uncleanness. What an indictment against the spirit of religion!

Babylon means 'confusion' having its roots in the Tower of Babel found in Genesis 11. It is here that God confused the tongues of humanity and produced so many different languages. As we travel the nations today in our mission ministry, we have always to deal with this Babylonian confusion of languages. In one trip, we have to translate into French or Spanish or German or Portuguese. Another trip takes us to the scores of dialects of the Philippine Islands, and yet another to the languages of Africa. How wonderful will be the time when we get into His Eternal Kingdom and we will all speak the same tongue. My husband's old grandfather was certain that we would all speak "Dutch" in heaven. A wonderful thing has happened with the coming of the Pentecostal Movement and the restoration of the 'Gift of Tongues' to the church. No matter where we are in the world, when a Chinaman or an African speaks in their heavenly language, a Spirit-filled believer can tell instantly it is the Holy Spirit as it is not even spoken with a brogue or an accent.

Verses 6-8:

6. *And I saw the woman drunken with the blood of the saints, and with the blood of the martyrs of Jesus; when I saw her, I wondered with great admiration (amazement).*

7. *And the angel said unto me, Wherefore didst thou marvel? I will tell thee the mystery of the woman, and of the beast that carrieth her, which hath the seven heads and ten horns.*

8. *The beast that thou sawest was, and is not; and shall ascend out of the bottomless pit, and go into perdition; and they that dwell on the earth shall wonder, whose names were not written in the book of life from the foundation of the world, when they behold the beast that was, and is not, and yet is.*

Now this woman, who represents *"that great city"*, is shown to be drunk with the blood of the saints and the martyrs of our Lord Jesus. There are two aspects to human blood. The first is the mortal, visible blood, which flows in everyone's veins. It will die with the body for the Scripture declares, *"the life of the flesh is in the blood."* (Lev. 17:11). Secondly, we find the immortal, invisible blood, which never dies. This means that when tyrants of the earth martyr God's people, the mortal visible blood is swallowed up by the ground. The invisible part of the blood, which never dies, cries unto the Lord God for vengeance.

"How long, O Lord, holy and true, dost Thou not judge and avenge our <u>blood</u> on them that dwell on the earth?" (Rev. 6:10).

It is this part of the blood that God pours back on the earth in judgment upon unrighteousness. The wicked have sown blood, therefore they must now reap blood. God said to Cain in Genesis 4:10. *"What hast thou done? The voice of thy brother's (Abel) blood(s) crieth unto me!"* The original Hebrew is in the plural confirming what I said.)

Now, the angel tells John about the mystery of the woman, who she is, and about the beast, who he is. We already discussed back in Chapter 13 who this beast, the anti-Christ, might really be. Go back there and read it again to refresh your mind. But now, *'who is this woman?'*

Verses 9,15,18:

9. *And here is the mind which hath wisdom. The seven heads are seven mountains on which the woman sitteth.*

15. *And he saith unto me, The waters which thou sawest, where the whore sitteth, are peoples, and multitudes, and nations, and tongues.*

18. *And the woman which thou sawest is <u>that great city</u> which reigneth over the kings of the earth.*

I deliberately chose to go to these three verses amidst this section because they particularly deal with *"the woman"* while the rest deal with the beast or the anti-Christ.

Here we find several important factors to understand exactly who is *'this scarlet woman'*.

1. She represents *"that great city"* spoken of ten times in Revelation, five of them in Chapter 8.

2. *"that great city"* is situated on seven mountains.

3. The *'waters'* where she sits represent all humanity whom give homage to *"that great city"*.

As I mentioned before, we will analyze *"that great city"* as we study Chapter 18 where it is recorded five times. As we do, it will give you a better understanding of this woman called 'The Great Whore of Revelation'.

The second allegory of which John had been speaking is that of the *"beast"* as we find it recorded here.

Verses 10-14,16,17:

10. *And there are seven kings; five are fallen, and one is, and the other is not yet come; and when he cometh he must continue a short space (3 ½ years).*

11. *And the beast that was, and is not, even he is the eighth, and is of the seven (the same spirit), and goeth into perdition.*

12. *And the ten horns which thou sawest are ten kings, which have received no kingdom as yet; but receive power as kings one hour (a short time) with the beast.*

13. *These have one mind, and shall give their power and strength unto the beast.*

14. *These shall make war with the Lamb, and the Lamb shall overcome them; for he is Lord of lords, and King of kings; and they that are with him are called and chosen and faithful!*

16. *And the ten horns which thou sawest upon the beast, these shall hate the whore, and shall make her desolate and naked, and shall eat her flesh, and burn her with fire.*

17. For God hath put in their hearts to fulfill his will, and to agree, and give their kingdom unto the beast, until the words of God shall be fulfilled.

These are some verses to try to decipher, but here goes.

It starts out with *"seven kings"* (Verse 10). These are thought to be the seven Gentile Kingdoms as revealed to Daniel the Prophet namely: Assyria, Egypt, Babylon, Medo-Persia, Greece, Rome, and finally, the One World Government. The first five of these worldly kingdoms have already fallen; the sixth still exists today in both religious and political form. The Roman Church and the Vatican is the only one on earth to have political power to the extent of having embassies from almost every nation on earth represented there. Watch the DVD "Of Angels and Demons" for an eye-opener. The seventh will appear in power at the time of the end.

Verse 11 tells us that the coming *"beast"*, the anti-Christ, is the eighth, but he is of the seven as to having the same spirit of taking over the earth. Just take a little look at history and the story is always the same. Be it Alexander the Great of Greece or Nero of Rome. Be it Adolf Hitler in more recent times or Stalin after him. All had the same spirit, to reign over the kings of the earth. Hallelujah! Only one will ever reign over the kings and the nations of the earth and His name is Jesus.

Verses 12 and 13 present us with the coming 'One world government' of the end-time. This body will give their power and homage to the *"beast"*, the anti-Christ, who will reign over them for just a *"short space"* (verse 10) and *"one hour"* (verse 12). God is just letting us know that he, the beast, doesn't have long to do his dirty work so we should not fear. Besides, when he and his followers in the one-world nations make the stupid mistake to *"make war with the Lamb"*, well that's it for *"the Lamb shall overcome them!"* (verse 14).

Note with me that there are three qualifications for those who will rule with the Lamb (verse 14).

"Called" - How wonderful to be assured that we have been called of the Lord to be with Him for all eternity and to rule and reign with Him as overcomers.

"Chosen" – Jesus said, *"Ye have not <u>chosen</u> me, but I have <u>chosen</u> you!"* (Emphasis added.) God has hand-picked those who will be by His side for all eternity. Oh, that we might prove ourselves to be worthy of that high and holy choosing.

"Faithful" – Paul said in First Corinthians 4:2, *"It is required in stewards that a man be found faithful."* The greatest words we will ever hear from our blessed Lord and Master are these. *"Well done thou good and faithful servant!"*

Finally, this chapter tells us how the one-world nations reacted in this short space of time. It says, *"these shall hate the whore"*. When we see in the next chapter who the whore, *"that great city"*, really is then you will see why they hated her and always have.

In studying Babylon, we must realize that this Babylon of Revelation 17 and 18 cannot be the literal Babylon of the Old Testament, which is our present day Iraq. The Babylon of the Book of Revelation has a 'spiritual' connotation and must be studied in a spiritual sense.

CHAPTER 18

THAT GREAT CITY

Verses 1-8:

1. *And after these things I saw another angel come down from heaven, having great power; and the earth was lightened with glory.*

2. *And he mightily with a strong voice, saying, Babylon <u>the great</u> <u>(city)</u> is fallen, is fallen, and is become the habitation of devils, and the hold of every foul spirit, and a cage of every unclean and hateful bird.*

3. *For all nations have drunk of the wine of the wrath of her fornication, and the kings of the earth have committed fornication with her, and the merchants of the earth are waxed rich through the abundance of her delicacies.*

4. *And I heard another voice from heaven, saying, Come out of her, my people, that ye be not partakers of her sins, and that ye receive not of her plagues.*

5. *For her sins have reached unto heaven, and God hath remembered her iniquities.*

6. *Reward her even as she rewarded you, and double unto her double according to her works; in the cup which she hath filled fill to her double.*

7. *How much she hath glorified herself, and lived deliciously, so much torment and sorrow give her; for she saith in her heart, I sit a queen, and am no widow, and shall see no sorrow.*

8. *Therefore shall her plagues come in one day, death, and mourning, and famine; and she shall be utterly burned with fire; for strong is the Lord God who judgeth her.*

As we read all of this we know more than ever that God will not be mocked by man or his spirit of religion. I am also convinced that much of what is written about the *"great city"* in this and the previous chapters is written in a spiritual sense. Why? Because she rejected the great and marvelous grace of our God in sending His Only Begotten Son to this world to redeem us from our sins and from an eternity in damnation. She turned her back on God's grace and went on in her old religious ways to 'save' herself.

So much has been written in so many books about this Babylon spoken of here in Revelation 17 and 18. What city on earth can it really be? Most evangelical commentators attribute Babylon to Rome, primarily because they feel that the Roman Church is apostate and *"the great whore"*. Many of these scholars had previously been Catholic or brought up in that faith so now have disdain for it. One of the reasons given for Rome as *"that great city"* and the Roman Church as the whore is because it speaks of the city as sitting on seven mountains.

"The seven heads (of the beast) are seven mountains on which the woman sitteth." (Rev. 17:10).

It is a fact that Rome does sit on seven hills or mountains and is called 'The Eternal City'. But look at this fact as well: Old Jerusalem, in existence much longer than Rome, also sits on seven hills. Brother Gene Little, who lives in Jerusalem, gave me a list of the seven hills or mountains of Jerusalem. Here they are: 1. Mount Hertzl 2. Mount Gilo 3. Mt. Zion 4. Mt. Scopus 5. Mt. Moriah 6. Mt. Olivet 7. Samuel's Mountain.

As we consider now the references to *"that great city"*, ponder them with me and see what conclusion you may draw from these texts.

1. *"the great city where also our Lord was crucified"* (11:8).

2. *"that great city made all nations drink of the wine of the wrath of her fornication"* (14:8).

3. *"the great city was divided into three parts and the cities of the nations fell"* (16:19).

4. *"that great city which reigneth over the kings of the earth"* (17:18).

5. *"Alas that great city, that mighty city, for in one hour is thy judgment come"* (18:10).

6. *"Alas that great city that was clothed in fine linen, and purple, and scarlet..."* (18:16).

7. *"What city is like unto this great city!"* (18:18).

8. *"Alas that great city wherein all were made rich...for in one hour is she made desolate"* (18:19)

9. *"Thus with violence shall that great city be thrown down"* (18:21).

10. *"And he carried me away in the Spirit, and showed me that great city, the holy New Jerusalem descending out of heaven from God!"* (21:10).

This last passage speaking of the *"great city"* is written after God makes *"all things new"* (21:5). It does not show us the Old Jerusalem now forsaken and set aside, but the "New Jerusalem" wherein dwells righteousness.

The one verse in all these that seems to really denote which city on earth was the *"great city"* is the verse found in Revelation 11:8. Speaking here of the 'Two Witnesses' who testify during 'The Great Tribulation', it says:, "*And their dead bodies shall lie in the street of the <u>great city</u>, which <u>spiritually</u> (not literally) is called Sodom and Egypt, <u>where also our Lord was crucified!</u>*"

In which city on this earth was our Lord Jesus crucified? Was it Rome or was it Old Jerusalem? This verse got me to thinking about this *"great city"*.

To our knowledge, our Jesus never went to Rome. It is possible He did, but there is no record found of this fact. The Mormon Church believes He visited North America and maybe other places on earth, but this is all conjecture without Biblical or historical fact.

Our Lord Jesus was crucified in the Old City of Jerusalem, which the Scripture here calls the *"great city"*.

The great political push of America and the E.U. nations in our day is to divide the City of Jerusalem back into its pre-1967 days. In this way, the eastern part of the city will belong to the Palestinians (formerly belonging to the Kingdom of Jordan). The western part of the city will belong to its rightful owners, the State of Israel. The Lord Himself under King David over 3,000 years ago, made Jerusalem the capital of Israel so who is man to change God's plan at this late era of time. Years ago, the United States Congress passed a resolution to move our embassy from Tel Aviv to Jerusalem. It has not been done to this day!

When the city of Old Jerusalem, referred to here as *"that great city"*, is brought into remembrance for her rejection of the Messiah, the Lord Jesus Christ, the justice of our Eternal God demands that He pass a sentence upon her. Jesus Himself declared this word:

And when he was come near, he beheld the city, and wept over it. Saying, If thou hadst known, even thou, at least in this thy day, the things which belong unto thy peace! But now they are hid from thine eyes. For the days shall come upon thee, that thine enemies shall cast a trench about thee, and compass thee round, and keep thee in on every side, And shall lay thee even with the ground, and thy children within thee; and they shall not leave in thee one stone upon another; because thou knewest not the time of thy visitation.

(Luke 19:41-44)

What an indictment against a city even by the Lord Himself. Oh, that we will never forget or let pass by us, our own *"time of visitation"*. Each of us in our lifetime has a time when God, in His Sovereign Grace, visits us with His mercy and goodness. I think back to those gracious times of visitation from the Lord in my own personal life and in that of our ministry over the past 60 years. Always know and be conscious of those times and never let them pass lightly.

The Prophet Zechariah describes Old Jerusalem thus, *"And in that day will I make Jerusalem a burdensome stone for all people; all that burden themselves with it shall be cut in pieces, though all the people of the earth be gathered together against it."* (Zech.12:3).

Who has prostituted herself anymore than has Rome with the very seat on earth of 'prostituted religion', but remember, that during the Great Tribulation, the anti-Christ does not sit in Rome or rule the earth for a short season from Rome, but from Old Jerusalem who allows his evil throne to be established there. Jesus earthly throne was rejected; that of the anti-Christ will be accepted!

While Jesus on earth ministered much in the Old City of Jerusalem, yet His words to that city were always words of warning and that of judgment to come. Being the Eternal God that He was, He knew the future and that which would come to pass in its day. His entire ministry was that of miracles among them. Yet they cried, *"Let his blood be on us and on our children!"* (Matt. 27:25). Jesus spoke prophetically to this city in His day when He said, *"I am come in My Father's name and ye receive me not; another shall come in his own name, him will ye receive."* (John 5:43). Jesus was speaking, of course, of the anti-Christ who was to come.

<u>Verses 9-19:</u>

9. *And the kings of the earth, who have committed fornication and lived deliciously with her, shall bewail her and lament for her, when they shall see the smoke of her burning,*

10. *Standing afar off for the fear of her torment, saying, Alas, alas <u>that great city</u> Babylon, that mighty city! For in one hour is thy judgment come.*

11. *And the merchants of the earth shall weep and mourn over her; for no man buyeth their merchandise any more;*

12. *The merchandise of gold, and silver, and precious stones, and of pearls, and fine linen, and purple, and silk, and scarlet, and all thy wood, and all manner vessels of ivory, and all manner vessels of most precious wood, and of brass, and iron, and marble.*

13. *And cinnamon, and odours, and ointments, and frankincense, and wine, and oil, and fine four, and wheat, and beasts, and sheep, and horses, and chariots, and slaves, and souls of men.*

14. *And the fruits that thy soul lusted after are departed from thee, and all things which were dainty and goodly are departed from thee, and thou shalt find them no more at all.*

15. *The merchants of these things, which were made rich by her, shall stand afar off for the fear of her torment, weeping and wailing.*

16. *And saying, Alas, alas <u>that great city</u>, that was clothed in fine linen, and purple, and scarlet, and decked with gold, and precious stones, and pearls!*

17. For in one hour so great riches is come to naught, And every shipmaster, and all the company in ships, and sailors, and as many as trade by the sea, stood afar off,

18. And cried when they saw the smoke of her burning, saying, What city is like unto <u>this great city</u>!

19. And they cast dust on their heads, and cried, weeping and wailing, saying, Alas, alas <u>that great city</u>, wherein were made rich all that had ships in the sea by reason of her costliness! For in one hour is she made desolate.

We have come to know that there is a two-fold spirit of Babylon in the world, that of 1) Ecclesiastical Babylon and 2) Economic Babylon. Both of these worldly systems will fall in the end to make room for the great Millennial Reign of our Lord and Savior, Jesus Christ.

These verses we have just seen speak of 'Economic Babylon' and her control of the world's wealth and finances which in the end will all collapse anyway.

Now, in the final verses of Chapter 18, we see the religious side of this Babylon spirit. As we read these verses, remember the words of our Lord in Luke 13 and Matthew 23.

And, behold, there are last which shall be first, and there are first which shall be last. The same day there came certain of the Pharisees, saying unto him, Get thee out, and depart hence, for Herod will kill thee. And Jesus said unto them, Go ye, and tell that fox, Behold, I cast out devils, and I do cures (healing) today and tomorrow, and <u>the third day</u> I shall be perfected (complete). Nevertheless I must walk today, and tomorrow, and the day following; for it cannot be that a prophet perish out of Jerusalem. O Jerusalem, Jerusalem, which killest the prophets, and stonest them that are sent unto thee; how often would I have gathered thy children together, as a hen doth gather her brood under her wings, *and ye would not! Behold, your house is left unto you desolate; and verily I say unto you, Ye shall not see me, until the time come when ye shall say, Blessed is he that cometh in the name of the Lord.*

(Luke 13:30-35)

Jesus said He would be *"casting out devils"* and *"doing cures"*, that is *"healing the sick"*, during His earthly ministry, but not only then. He uses a prophetic term here in Luke when He says, *"today and tomorrow"*. The Apostle Peter tells us *"one day is with the Lord as a thousand years and a thousand years as one day."* This is found in Second Peter 3:8. With this in mind, we see that Jesus was saying that for the next two thousand years I am going to be *"casting out devils and healing the sick"* through My True Church. By the way, this was His commission to the church! Jesus then makes an incredible prophetic statement before He pronounces this end-time judgment upon Old Jerusalem. He says, *"and on the THIRD DAY I shall be perfected!"*

God gave me a message some years ago about this subject of *'The Third Day'* and I preached it several times, but the timing of it was not right. This was back in late 80's when they were predicting the time of the Lord's coming. One man even gave us 88 reasons why He was coming in 1988. Well, we are some years now into the New Millennium and Christ has still not returned. It has been two thousand years since Jesus spoke these words. We are now in the morning of *"the third day"* when He said that His work would be perfected or finished.

Beloved, we may not have much longer to wait. Let's be ready for that great *'Third Day'* as it tells us in Exodus 19:10,11,16, *"And the Lord said unto Moses, Go unto the people, and sanctify them today and tomorrow, and let them wash their clothes. And be ready against the third day; for the third day THE LORD WILL COME DOWN...And it came to pass on the third day in the morning!"*

I am now preaching this vital message once again as it is time for all of it to come to pass. I am hoping soon to get the message, *The Morning of the Third Day*, into book form as well.

Verses 20-24:

20. *Rejoice over her, thou heaven, and ye holy apostles and prophets; for God hath avenged you on her.*

21. *And a mighty angel took up a stone like a great millstone, and cast it into the sea, saying, Thus with violence shall that great city Babylon be thrown down, and shall be found no more at all.*

22. *And the voice of harpers, and musicians, and of pipers, and trumpeters, shall be heard no more at all in thee; and no craftsman, of whatever craft he be, shall be found any more in thee; and the sound of a millstone shall be heard no more at all in thee;*

23. *And the light of a candle shall shine no more at all in thee; and the voice of the bridegroom and of the bride shall be heard no more at all in thee; for they merchants were the great men of the earth; for by thy sorceries were all nations deceived.*

24. *And in her was found the blood of prophets, and of saints, and of all that were slain upon the earth.*

Where did this all take place? *"in that great city where also our Lord was crucified!"* (Rev. 11:8).

As I was about to close the writing of Chapter 18, the Lord reminded me that 'any city that rejects the true Lord Jesus and accepts a form of religion instead' could in essence be called *"that great city"*. This could include Rome, the most religious city in the world as regards Christianity in general. Cities in India are totally given to Hindu idolatry. Other cities in Asia are totally given to Buddhist idolatry. Mecca is given totally to Muslim idolatry. So it is that there are so-called 'great cities' by their own religion.

Oh, what a difference between 'religion' and the true worship of our Lord Jesus Christ which is done in simplicity without the fanfare and hoopla of men's doings. While Jesus walked His pilgrim journey here below, He strongly emphasized one thing, among many others of course, so it appears in all of the synoptic gospels of Matthew, Mark and Luke. *"Beware of the leaven of the Pharisees!"*

Pharisaical religion, when injected into pure religion, will eventually leaven or affect the entire thing so it becomes a duke's mixture of none affect. Jesus went on to say this:

"Thus have ye made the commandment of God of none effect by your tradition." (Matt. 15:6).

"Making the word of God of none effect through your tradition." (Mark 7:13).

Let us not be a part of the system of Old Jerusalem, but citizens of that *"New Jerusalem coming down from God out of heaven!"* (Rev. 21:2).

CHAPTER 19

THE MARRIAGE OF THE LAMB

Verses 1-9:

1. *And after these things I heard a great voice of much people in heaven, saying, Alleluia, Salvation, and glory, and honour, and power, unto the Lord our God;*

2. *For true and righteous are his judgments; for he hath judged the great whore, which did corrupt the earth with her fornication, and hath avenged the blood of his servants at her hand.*

3. *And again they said, Alleluia, And her smoke rose up forever and ever.*

4. *And the four and twenty elders and the four beasts (living creatures) fell down and worshipped God that sat on the throne, saying, Amen; Allelujah!*

5. *And a voice came out of the throne, saying, Praise our God, all ye his servants, and ye that fear him, both small and great.*

6. *And I heard as it were the voice of a great multitude, and as the voice of many waters, and as the voice of mighty thunderings, saying, Allelujah; for the Lord God omnipotent reigneth.*

7. *Let us be glad and rejoice, and give honour to him; for the <u>marriage of the Lamb</u> is come, and his wife hath made herself ready.*

8. *And to her was granted that she should be arrayed in fine linen, clean and white, for the fine linen is the righteousness of saints.*

9. *And he saith unto me, Write, Blessed are they which are called unto the <u>marriage supper of the Lamb</u>. And he saith unto me, These are the true saying of God.*

These wonderful verses always remind me of an old R.E. Winsett song we sang so often in years past.

We shall all rise to meet Him,
We shall all go to greet Him,
In the morning when the dead in Christ shall rise.
We shall all rise to meet Him,
We shall all go to greet Him,
And we'll have the marriage supper up in the skies.

We miss all of those good old songs that taught us about the joys and glories of heaven.

We see in these verses above that there were three groups of 'saints' in heaven. All of them were a part of that glorious assembly of the redeemed. It is just that there were definite distinctions as to their position in God's Eternal Kingdom. Look at these with me.

The Great Multitude – clothed in *"WHITE ROBES"*
The 24 Elders – clothed in *"WHITE RAIMENT"*
The Lamb's Wife – clothed in *"WHITE LINEN"*

Throughout God's Word a clear distinction is made of these redeemed groups of people. We see them here at the Marriage Supper of the Lamb referred to as:

The Guests (The Great Multitude) at the marriage.
The Attendants (The Elders/Governors).
The Bride Herself (The Lamb's wife).

No one has ever been to a marriage where everyone there was the bride. There are guests, there are the attendants (best man, groomsmen, maid-of-honor, bridesmaids) and then there is the bride herself. So will it be in God's Eternal Kingdom.

Jesus taught us this in His parables. First, in Matthew 22 He taught us the parable of 'the marriage of the king's son'. In it He declares these words, *"And the wedding was furnished with GUESTS"* (Matt. 22:10).

Three chapters later He taught us about the 'virgins' who were the *'bridesmaids'* or the ATTENDANTS to the bride. Remember, *"they ALL slumbered and slept."* This included even the 'wise ones'. It was the bride herself, who could not sleep in anticipation of her coming bridegroom. She made the cry, *"Behold, the bridegroom cometh!"* (Matt. 25:6).

Jesus spoke in Matthew 13:23 and again in Mark 6:8 to those in the Eternal Kingdom who would be:

Thirty-fold Sixty-fold Hundred-fold

The Apostle Paul in writing about the resurrection of the dead and eternity had this to say about these three groups. *"There is one glory of the SUN, and another glory of the MOON, and another glory of the STARS; for one star differeth from another star in glory. So also is the resurrection of the dead!"* (1 Cor. 15:41,42).

We have said before that God always seems to work in 'threes' in keeping with His Eternal Being as Father, Word/Son, and Holy Spirit. He thus made us as a three-fold nature being with spirit, soul and body.

There are three different Greek words in the Scriptures to describe the three kinds of apparel to be worn in eternity.

WHITE ROBES *'stole'* a long garment or an outer covering.[1]

WHITE RAIMENT *'himation'* a special apparel or vesture.[2]

WHITE LINEN *'bussos'* to be made of fine twined linen.[3]

---

[1] (Strong's #4749)
[2] (Strong's #2440)
[3] (Strong's #1040)

Our God is always righteous and true and, even in His eternal dealings with the redeemed, He will reward us according to the stature we have gained in Him while on our earthly journey. Remember, we came from eternity and we are going back to eternity. We only dwell a little while in this space called 'time'.

It would not be fair for someone who had just been saved or accepted Jesus' blood as atonement for their sins, to receive the same rewards and position in the Eternal Kingdom as one who had served God with all their might throughout their lifetime. True, everyone who loves the Lord will be happy and blessed in eternity, but not all will have the same position. The Word teaches us this as to these blessed eternal appointments. Those in eternity will be:

SERVANTS – *"Praise our God, all ye his servants." "And his servants shall serve him." "They serve him day and night."* (Rev. 19:5; 22:3; 7:15).

What a joy it will be to serve the Lord who redeemed us by His own blood for all eternity. Not only do they serve, but they also worship God and the Lamb forever and ever.

GOVERNORS – These are found in the 24 Elders, a representative number of those who are clothed in 'white raiment'. This group will be those who manage the affairs of this Eternal Kingdom. They are referred to twelve times in the Book of Revelation.

THE BRIDE – She is one with her Bridegroom and was bonded to Him during her walk on earth as she totally sold out to the Lord and His will for her life. She now enjoys the reward of all the sacrifices she made in her earthly journey to be one in the throne with Him who is her beloved. This was Jesus' own promise to her, His bride, who are those who *"overcome"* in this life – "the world, the flesh, and the devil".

"To him that overcometh will I grant to <u>sit with me in my throne</u>, even as I also overcame and am set down with my Father in his throne." (Rev. 3:21).

We can be overcomers through the grace that He has given us. *"By the blood of the Lamb and the word of our testimony"* is what Revelation 12:11 has promised us.

Verse 10:

And I fell at this feet to worship him. And he said unto me, See thou do it not; I am thy fellowservant, and of thy brethren that have the testimony of Jesus; worship God; for the testimony of Jesus is the spirit of prophecy.

John is here told by the Heavenly Angel, who has escorted him through the splendors of heaven and shown him the terrors of the Great Tribulation, not to worship him, but very distinctly says, *"worship God"*. In our travels to the nations, one of the most unusual "Christian" groups of people we found was in Nigeria, Africa. They literally worshipped angels along with the Lord. Angel statues and angelic replicas were everywhere and they did not seem to think anything of it. Of course, many traditional churches worship everything from saints of old, relics of the church and even the mother of our Lord.

Recently, while we were in Israel at the famous Church of St. Anne, we were told that prayers to St. Anne availed much because Jesus would honor His grandmother more than just any old saint. Anne was purported to be the mother of the Blessed Virgin. We always love to sing as a group in this old church as the acoustics are near perfect and resound so beautifully. We always take our tour group up on the altar and form a choir. Every time we draw a crowd as we worship the Lord in Spirit and in truth.

"The Testimony of Jesus" - The Word here says that it is the *'spirit of prophecy'*. This being the case, how very important it is that we adhere to Paul's admonition in First Thessalonians 5:20, *"Despise not prophesyings!"* Three whole chapters of Paul's inspired writings under the anointing of the Holy Spirit, were written primarily about 'prophesying' – First Corinthians 12, 13 and 14. If it is that important to the Holy Spirit, then it should be equally as important to the church today. This is the day of the prophetic and God is saying some awesome things to His Church. Let's take heed to the voice of the prophets that He has put in our land.

THE WHITE HORSE ARMY

Verses 11-16:

11. *And I saw heaven opened, and behold a <u>white horse</u>; and he that sat upon him was called Faithful and True, and in righteousness he doth judge and make war.*

12. *His eyes were as a flame of fire, and on his head were many crowns; and he had a name written, that no man knew, but he himself.*

13. *And he was clothed with a vesture dipped in blood; and his name is called The Word of God.*

14. *And the armies which were in heaven followed him upon <u>white horses</u>, clothed in fine linen, white and clean.*

15. *And out of his mouth goeth a sharp sword, that with it he should smite the nations; and he shall rule them with a rod of iron; and he treadeth the winepress of the fierceness and wrath of Almighty God.*

16. *And he hath on his vesture and on his thigh a name written, KING OF KINGS, AND LORD OF LORDS!*

We now see this great army of the saints in heaven riding upon white horses and following the Lord Jesus upon His White Horse. Remember our study back in Chapter 6 when we saw the first horseman of the Apocalypse and he was also riding a white horse. I told you then that the horseman there was not the Lord Jesus, but rather the anti-Christ who imitates our Lord. Here is the real Jesus coming as Jude wrote in his epistle saying, *"Behold, the Lord cometh with ten thousands of his saints."* (Jude 14).

What a picture is portrayed here in Chapter 19 of our wonderful Lord. He is called in these few verses:

1. Faithful and True.
2. The righteous judge.
3. The Word of God.
4. King of Kings.
5. Lord of Lords.

As He comes back with His overcoming saints, the Bible tells us this.

"And his feet shall stand in that day upon the Mount of Olives, which is before Jerusalem on the east, and the Mount of Olives shall cleave in the midst thereof toward the east and toward the west, and there shall be a very great valley; and half of the mountain shall remove toward the north, and half of it toward the south...and the Lord my God shall come, and all the saints with thee...and it shall be in that day that living waters shall go out from Jerusalem...and the Lord shall be King over all the earth; in that day there shall be ONE LORD, and his name one." (Zech. 14:4-9).

What a picture of that glorious day when the Lord shall return to earth. This is not the rapture or the 'catching away' of the overcoming church. This is when Jesus actually returns physically and literally to this old earth some 3½ years after the 'catching away'.

In that day, it will be more than a song like 'What a Day That Will Be'. It will be a reality!

Verses 17-21:

17. *And I saw an angel standing in the sun; and he cried with a loud voice, saying to all the fowls that fly in the midst of heaven, Come and gather yourselves together unto the supper of the great God.*

18. *That ye may eat of the flesh of kings, and the flesh of captains, and the flesh of mighty men, and the flesh of horses, and of them that sit on them, and the flesh of all men, both free and bond, both small and great.*

19. *And I saw the beast (anti-Christ), and the kings of the earth, and their armies, gathered together to make war against him that sat on the (white) horse, and against his army.*

20. *And the beast was taken, and with him the false prophet that wrought (false) miracles before him, with which he deceived them that had received the mark of the beast, and them that worshipped his image. These were both cast alive into the lake of fire burning with brimstone.*

21. *And the remnant were slain with the sword of him that sat upon the (white) horse, which sword proceeded out of his mouth; and all the fowls were filled with their flesh.* (Emphasis added).

Here we see the results of the Battle of Armageddon when the Lord returns on His White Horse with the armies of heaven to fight against the anti-Christ and his earthly armies. We know that no earthly army can stand against a heavenly one so the outcome is quite obvious. The armies of heaven already have glorified eternal bodies so they cannot be killed. Their commander-in-chief is none other than King Jesus and already is eternal so . . .the fowls of the air have their fill on the dead flesh in the Valley of Megiddo.

Up until this time, the *'lake of fire'* is an uninhabited place. I know we hear the stories of those who have died in their sins and have gone to this place, but they are only looking to what the future will be. No one is now in this *'lake of fire'*. God in His

Eternal Justice cannot rightfully sentence anyone to 'eternal hell' until they have first been tried before His Great White Throne. This does not take place until after the millennium as we find in Revelation 20.

It is at this judgment seat that those whose names are not written in the Lamb's Book of Life will be tried. They then will find their fate in this eternal hell called the *'lake of fire'*. This brings up a real question. Where then are those who die now without the Lord Jesus Christ? They have to be in a 'waiting place' called in the Scriptures *"hades"*, a place of total separation from God awaiting His judgment day. Perhaps knowing their eternal fate already is like waiting on death row for inmates condemned to die.

The first two to be cast into the *'lake of fire'* are the beast, who is the anti-Christ, and his false prophet. This is quite clear from our text in verse 20. And they will be *"cast alive into the lake of fire"*. To say they deserve it is putting it mildly.

CHAPTER 20

THE MILLENIUM

Verses 1-6:

1. And I saw an angel come down from heaven, having the key of the bottomless pit and a great chain in his hand.

2. And he laid hold on the dragon, that old serpent, which is the Devil and Satan, and bound him a <u>thousand years,</u>

3. And cast him into the bottomless pit, and shut him up, and set a seal upon him, that he should deceive the nations no more, till the <u>thousand years</u> should be fulfilled; and after that he must be loosed for a little season.

4. And I saw thrones, and they sat upon them, and judgment was given unto them; and I saw the souls of them that were beheaded for the witness of Jesus, and for the Word of God, and which had not worshipped the beast, neither his image, neither had received his mark upon their foreheads, or in their hands, and they lived and reigned with Christ a <u>thousand years.</u>

5. But the rest of the dead lived not again until the <u>thousand years</u> were finished. This is the first resurrection.

6. Blessed and holy is he that hath part in the first resurrection; on such the second death hath no power, but they shall be priests of God and of Christ, and shall reign with him a <u>thousand years.</u>

What an unusual portion of Scripture! Up until this time little or no mention of this "thousand years" is spoken of in the Bible. Now, we have this term repeated several times in this one chapter. The church world is divided on the subject of the

'Millennium'. The word from the Latin simply means 'One Thousand Years'. There are three religious schools of thought about this thousand-year period mentioned here in the Bible.

Pre-millennial – This is the belief of most evangelical and Full Gospel churches and scholars. This doctrine simply states that the *"thousand years"* is an actual and literal period of 1,000 years during which Satan will be bound and Christ will reign upon the earth with His saints. An old gospel hymn we used to sing expresses it like this:

> I am watching for the coming of that glad millennial day,
> When our blessed Lord shall come and catch His waiting Bride away.
> Oh, my heart is filled with rapture as I labor, watch and pray,
> For our Lord is coming back to earth again.
>
> Oh, our Lord is coming back to earth again,
> Yes, our Lord is coming back to earth again.
> Satan will be bound a thousand years;
> We'll have no tempter then,
> When our Jesus shall come back to earth again.

A-millennial – This theory is taught and believed by many of the Reformation churches that came into being during the great Reformation of the mid 1500's. Because of the controversy of this doctrine, many scholars of that day did not even believe that the Book of Revelation should have been in the Canon of Scripture. A-millennialism teaches that this is just a figure of speech and no such thing as literal millennium was ever in the mind of God.

My husband was born and raised in the Reformed faith and as such was taught the A-millennial doctrine from his youth. Somehow it never stuck in his spirit so when he met up with the young people from the Pentecostal Church, he somehow just thought the idea of Pre-millennialism was the right one. As youth leader of his Reformed Church, he invited one of the girls from his newfound church to come and teach the young people of his historic church about the Second Coming including the teaching about the Millennium. No little stir was created as Bob was called before the elders to try to explain how he had allowed false doctrine to be taught in his youth group.

Post-millennial – I have always felt this theory to be rather absurd considering the degenerating condition of the world today. The Post-millennialists believe that the world is going to get better and better and finally the 'good earth' is going to be handed over to Jesus. Think again if this is your idea because all the teaching of Scripture lets us know that *"in the last days"* things are going to get worse and worse, not better and better.

Let's take a look at some of things that will happen during this thousand year period called *'The Millennium'*.

- Satan will be bound and cast into the bottomless pit.
- The overcomers will live and reign with Christ.
- Those who are in this period are blessed having been part of the First Resurrection.
- They will be priests unto God during the Millennium.

In addition to the promises of this text, there are the prophetic promises given by the Old Testament for the day of the reign of Christ, the Messiah, upon the earth.

"They shall not hurt nor destroy in all my holy mountain; for the earth shall be full of the knowledge of the Lord, as the waters cover the sea." (Isa. 11:9).

"The wolf also shall dwell with the lamb, and the leopard shall lie down with the kid; and the calf and the young lion and the fatling together; and a little child shall lead them." (Isa. 11:6,7).

"In that day living waters shall go out from Jerusalem...And the Lord shall be King over all the earth; in that day there shall be one Lord, and His name one...Jerusalem shall be safely inhabited!" (Zech. 14:8,9).

"In that day shall the branch of the Lord be beautiful and glorious, and the fruit of the earth shall be excellent and comely...And the Lord will create upon every dwelling place of Mount Zion, and upon her assemblies, a cloud and smoke by day, and the shining of a flaming fire by night (the Shekinah Glory of the Lord during the Millennium)." (Isa. 4:1,5).

Along with these and other Scripture passages referring to a coming millennium, the Prophet Ezekiel speaks of a Millennial Temple that shall be built during the coming thousand-year reign of Christ from *"the throne of His father David"*.

SATAN LOOSED FOR A SHORT TIME

There is an old saying that all good things must come to an end. So it is with the Millennial Reign of the Lord Jesus. However, this period only ends in total victory over Satan who is loosed for a little season from his prison only to go to a far worse place.

Verses 7-10:

7. *And when the <u>thousand years</u> are expired, Satan shall be loosed out of his prison.*

8. *And shall go out to deceive the nations which are in the four quarters of the earth, Gog and Magog, to gather them together to battle; the number of whom is as the sand of the sea.*

9. *And they went up on the breadth of the earth, and compassed the camp of the saints about, and the beloved city; and fire came down from God out of heaven, and devoured them.*

10. *And the devil that deceived them was cast into the lake of fire and brimstone, where the beast and the false prophet are (already), and shall be tormented day and night forever and ever*

Why in the world would God allow the enemy to be loosed out of his prison for a little while? As I thought about this, I realized that those upon the Millennial Earth had never really been tempted toward sin or evil. Christ was reigning in righteousness so there was no tempter or temptation. Now, for the first time, those born upon the earth during the Millennium would have a chance to choose between good and evil. Satan, it says, went out *"to deceive the nations"*. Those saints who had returned with Christ on white horses to *"rule and reign with him"* were compassed about by Satan, but to no avail. God's fire devoured them all!

Prior to the thousand years, the beast and the false prophet had already been cast into the *"lake of fire"*. They were the very first to ever be banished to that place. It was empty before they were condemned there forever. Now, the arch-enemy of the church and God's people, old 'slew-foot', satan himself, is cast in along with them. They all deserve each other for sure. And, be assured, there is no way out of that place.

THE GREAT WHITE THRONE

Verses 11-15:

11. *And I saw a <u>great white throne</u>, and him that sat on it, from whose face the earth and the heaven fled away; and there was found no place for them.*

12. And I saw the dead, small and great, stand before God; and the books were opened; and another book was opened which is the book of life, and the dead were judged out of those things which were written in the books, according to their works.

13. And the sea gave up the dead which were in it; and death and hell (hades) delivered up the dead which were in them; and they were judged every man according to their works.

14. And death and hell (hades) were cast into the lake of fire. This is the second death.

15. And whosoever was not found written in the book of life was cast into the lake of fire.

It has been said, "Those who are only born once will die twice; but those who have been born twice will only die once." This statement is so true as to what we read here. Those who have been *"born again, not of corruptible seed, but of incorruptible by the word of God, which liveth and abideth forever."* (1 Pet.1:23) will never have to die the *"second death"*. Those who have never experienced the 'new birth' are destined to face the *"second death"*.

It is interesting to note that there are several judgments mentioned in the Word of God. Among them are:

- *The judgment of believer's sins.* This took place some 2,000 years ago at Calvary where our Jesus paid the price for the sins of all who believe upon Him.

- *The believer's self-judgment.* We read the words of the Apostle Paul in First Corinthians 11:31, *"If we would judge ourselves, we should not be judged."*

- *The judgment of believer's works.* *"For we must all appear before the judgment seat of Christ."* Paul's words in Second Corinthians 5:10.

- *The judgment of the nations.* "*When the Son of Man shall come in his glory, and all the holy angels with him, then shall he sit upon the throne of his glory; And before him shall be gathered all nations; and he shall separate them one from another, as a shepherd divideth his sheep from the goats.*" (Matt. 25:31,32).

- *The judgment of Israel at Christ's coming.* "*But who may abide the day of his coming? And who shall stand when he appeareth?...He shall sit (in judgment) as a refiner and purifier of silver, and he shall purify the sons of Levi, and purge them as gold and silver.*" (Mal. 3:2,3).

- *The judgment of fallen angels.* "*And the angels which kept not their first estate, but left their own habitation, he hath reserved in everlasting chains under darkness unto the judgment of the great day.*" (Jude 6).

Paul said of believers, "*Know ye not that we shall judge angels?*" (1 Cor. 6:3).

- *The Great White Throne judgment.* "*And I saw a great white throne...And I saw the dead, small and great, stand before God; and the books were opened.*" (Rev. 20:11,12).

We are now at this final judgment following which the earth will be renovated by fire and we will see the glorious "*new heaven and new earth*" which our God shall miraculously create by the word of His power. The Apostle Peter tells about this in Second Peter 3:10-13.

"*The heavens shall pass away with a great noise, and the elements shall melt with fervent heat, the earth also and the works that are therein shall be burned up. Seeing then that all these things will be dissolved, what manner of persons ought ye to be in all holy conversation and godliness. Looking for and hasting unto the coming of the day of God, wherein the heavens being on fire shall be dissolved, and the elements shall melt with fervent heat? Nevertheless we, according to his promise, look for new heavens and a new earth, wherein dwelleth righteousness."*

In the final two chapters of Revelation, we are going to see the beauty and glory of the three places of eternal abode for all believers of all ages.

'The New Heaven'

'The New Earth'

'The New Holy City'

CHAPTER 21

ALL THINGS NEW

Verses 1-5:

1. And I saw a <u>new heaven</u> and a <u>new earth</u>; for the first heaven and the first earth were passed away; and there was no more sea.

2. And I John saw the holy city, <u>new Jerusalem</u>, coming down from God out of heaven, prepared as a bride adorned for her husband.

3. And I heard a great voice out of heaven saying, Behold, the tabernacle of God is with men, and he will dwell with them, and they shall be his people, and God himself shall be with them, and be their God.

4. And God shall wipe away all tears from their eyes; and there shall be no more death, neither sorrow, nor crying, neither shall there be any more pain; for the former things are passed away.

5. And he that sat upon the throne said, Behold, I make <u>ALL THINGS NEW</u>. And he said unto me, Write: for these words are true and faithful.

Eternity has now come into view. Time has been declared to be no more. We are now back with God from whence we came in the first place. *"All things were made by him, and without him was not anything made that was made!"* (John 1:3).

"ALL THINGS NEW" is the theme of Revelation 21. We see here the long-awaited three-fold abode of all the righteous from the beginning of time until its ending.

- *"The New Heaven"* – The abode of the saints of all ages clothed in "White Robes".

- *"The New Earth"* – Where the righteous nations will dwell under the everlasting rulership of those clothed in special governmental garments of "White Raiment".

- *"The New Jerusalem"* also called that "New City".

Here in the midst of that Eternal City is the throne of God and the Lamb, which is the seat of God's Everlasting Government. Ruling with Him is His Eternal Bride clothed in "White Linen".

Along with all things new, we see that the old things have passed away. In eternity there will be:

- *'no more tears'* – These were the tears of trouble which this old world has always afforded, now gone forever!

- *'no more death'* – *"It is appointed unto man once to die."* (Heb. 9:27). Not anymore!

- *'no more sorrow'* – Sorrow will not even be a memory of the old that all of us had down here.

- *'no more crying'* – *"And God shall wipe away all tears from their eyes!"* (Verse 4).

- *'no more pain'* – Everyone hates pain both physical and emotional. It, too, will be gone.

- *'no more growing old'* – Aging is a process that none can avoid. Men have always sought for that mystical, proverbial 'Fountain of Youth'.

We will have eternal youth forever over there. Those that have been blessed to visit eternity in the Spirit, have always had one thing to say about those they saw their including old friends and loved ones. No one was ever 'old'. Though they were old when they died, now they have eternal youth. Most were somewhere in their mid-thirties. Could it be perhaps because that was the earthly age of Jesus when He returned to His eternal glory?

Verses 6-8:

6. *And he said unto me, It is done. I am Alpha and Omega, the beginning and the end. I will give unto him that is athirst of the fountain of the water of life freely.*

7. *He that overcometh shall inherit all things; and I will be his God, and he shall be my son.*

8. *But the fearful, and unbelieving, and the abominable, and murderers, and whoremongers, and sorcerers, and idolaters, and all liars, shall have their part in the lake which burneth with fire and brimstone; which is the second death.*

Again, we see these words *"It is done"* that we saw back in Chapter 16. These words once again speak of the finality of God's Word. When He says something is done, it is done!

As repeated before in Revelation and throughout the Scriptures, the identity of the Lord Jesus is revealed in these words, *"Alpha and Omega, the beginning and the end!"* It also tells us in Revelation 1:11 that Jesus is *"the first and the last"* and I like to add, 'everything in between'. That's our Jesus, *"the author and finisher"*.

Here in this passage, we see another reference to the *"overcomers"* and God's promise to them here is that they *"shall inherit all things"* (verse 7). Ten times in the epistles we are told that *"we are heirs and joint-heirs"* with Him. It is good to strive to be an overcomer with all of these promises given to us.

Verse 8 of this section is a warning to all who read of the fate of those who fit the categories mentioned here. They will have part in the same place as the beast and the false prophet as well as the devil himself – the eternal *"lake of fire"*. Let's be overcomers!

THE HOLY CITY

Verses 9-11:

9. *And there came unto me one of the seven angels which had the seven vials full of the seven last plagues, and talked with me, saying, Come hither, I will shew thee the bride, the Lamb's wife.*

10. *And he carried me away in the spirit to a great and high mountain, and shewed me that great city, the holy Jerusalem, descending out of heaven from God.*

11. *Having the glory of God; and her light was like unto stone most precious, even like a jasper stone, clear as crystal.*

The angel told John that he would show him *"the bride, the Lamb's wife"*. Instead he showed him *"that great city, the holy Jerusalem"*. My immediate question was "Why a city, not a lovely woman?" It is because the "New City" is a picture of the bride in all her glory. In the rest of this chapter we will see 'her' walls, gates, foundations, and building. In its beauty, look for the beauty of the 'Bride of Christ' that she represents. Also remember that this city will be the eternal habitation of the bride who will be clothed in *"White Linen"*.

Verse 11 speaks of the *"jasper stone, clear as crystal"*. We saw this stone back in Chapter 4 as belonging to the Tribe of Benjamin, the last of Israel's sons, whose name means 'Son of my right hand'. Again, it is representative of our Lord Jesus as Hebrews 1:3 says, *"Who being the brightness of his glory, and the express image of his person, and upholding all things by the word of his power, when he had by himself purged our sins, sat down on the right hand of the Majesty on high!"*

We are now going to look at 'her' walls, 'her' gates, 'her' foundations, and 'her' building in the following verses of this chapter.

HER WALLS

Verses 12,14,15,17,18:

12. And had a <u>wall</u> great and high...

14. And the <u>wall</u> of the city had twelve foundations...

15. To measure the city...and the <u>wall</u> thereof.

17. And he measured the <u>wall</u> thereof, an hundred and forty and four cubits, according to the measure of a man, that is, of the angel.

18. And the building of the <u>wall</u> of it was of jasper and the city was pure gold, like unto clear glass.

These verses are descriptive of the *'walls'* of the city.
- The walls were great and high.
- The walls had twelve foundations.
- The walls were measured by the angel.
- The walls were like a cube in measurement.
- The walls were made of jasper-like crystal.

HER GATES

Verses 12,13,15,21,25:

12. And had twelve <u>gates</u>, and at the <u>gates</u> twelve angels, and names written thereon, which are the names of the twelve tribes of the children of Israel;

13. On the east three <u>gates</u>; on the north three <u>gates</u>; on the south three <u>gates</u>; and on the west three <u>gates</u>.

15. And he that talked with me had a golden reed to measure the city, and the <u>gates</u> thereof.

21. *And the twelve gates were twelve pearls; every several gate was one pearl.*

25. *And the gates of it shall not be shut at all by day; for there shall be no night there.*

Now, we see the description of the 'gates' of the city:

- The gates were twelve in number.
- At each gate there was a guardian angel.
- Each gate had the name of one of the twelve tribes of Israel.
- The gates were measured by the angel.
- The gates were made each of one great pearl.
- The gates were never shut.

HER FOUNDATIONS

Verses 14,19,20:

14. *And the wall of the city had twelve foundations, and in them the names of the twelve apostles of the Lamb.*

19. *And the foundations of the wall of the city were garnished with all manner of precious stones. The first foundation was jasper; the second, sapphire; the third, a chalcedony; the fourth, an emerald.*

20. *The fifth, sardonyx; the sixth, sardius; the seventh, chrysolyte; the eighth, beryl; the ninth, a topaz; the tenth, a chrysoprasus; the eleventh, a jacinth; the twelfth, an amethyst.*

The following things are told us about the 'foundations' of this Holy City:

- There were twelve foundations in this city.
- In them were the names of the twelve apostles of the Lamb.
- They were garnished with precious stones.

You will remember with me that our father Abraham was looking way back then for that city.

"By faith he sojourned in the land of promise, as in a strange country, dwelling in tabernacles with Isaac and Jacob, the heirs with him of the same promise; For he looked for a city which hath FOUNDATIONS whose builder and maker is God!" (Heb.11:9,10).

THE BUILDING OF THE CITY

Verses 15,16:

15. *And he that talked with me had a golden reed to measure the city.*

16. *And the city lieth foursquare, and the length is as large as the breadth; and he measured the city with the reed, twelve thousand furlongs. The length and the breadth and the height of it are equal.*

The New Jerusalem, the city built *"foursquare"*. It appears from this verse that the New City is a 'cube' for all dimensions of it are equal – 1,500 miles wide, 1,500 miles long, and 1,500 miles high.

Wow! What a city! It goes on further to describe this city in the final verses of this chapter.

Verses 22-27:

22. *And I saw no temple therein; for the Lord God Almighty and the Lamb are the temple of it.*

23. *And the city had no need of the sun, neither of the moon, to shine in it; for the glory of God did lighten it, and the Lamb is the light thereof.*

24. *And the nations of them which are saved shall walk in the light of it; and the kings of the earth do bring their glory and honour into it.*

25. *And the gates of it shall not be shut at all by day; for there is no night there.*

26. *And they shall bring the glory and honour of the nations into it.*

27. *And there shall in no wise enter into it any thing that defileth, neither whatsoever worketh abomination, or maketh a lie; but they which are written in the Lamb's book of life.*

In Verse 22 we see that there is *"no temple"* in the New City. Temples are places of worship, but in the New City, we will worship the Lord God directly so He Himself is the temple of that city.

In Verse 23, we note that the New City had no need of the lights that our Father originally created, that is, the sun, moon and stars. He is greater than any of His creation so the Lamb is the eternal light of the New City.

In our old "Melodies of Praise" hymnal, a song speaks about this beautiful city. The chorus goes like this:

> In that city where the Lamb is the light;
> In the city where there cometh no night.
> I've a mansion over there,
> And when free from toil and care,
> I am going where the Lamb is the light.

In the final verses of Chapter 21, we read about 'nations' on the New Earth. These *"nations of them which are saved"* are going to be eternally blessed because of the New City.

- They will live in the light of the Holy City.
- The kings will bring their glory and honor into it.
- The gates of the New City will never be shut.
- Only the redeemed will be able to enter there.

- The leaves of the Tree of Life will be for the eternal healing of the saved nations upon the New Earth. (Rev.22:2).

Very dear pastor friends of ours, Pastors Wm. Carl and Irma L. Brown from Louisville, Kentucky wrote the most wonderful song about 'The New City'. They are great songwriters and, with their permission, I am sharing it here with you. It starts out with the chorus.

> I've got that New City, New City on my mind;
> I've got that New City, New City on my mind.
> If you wanna go there; if you wanna go there
> Come along with me.
> I've got that New City, New City on my mind.
>
> It's got walls of jasper, street of gold,
> And gates of pearl.
> I'm going to a city, a city out of this world.
> Where the crystal river flows,
> And the tree of life stands there.
> I'm going to a city, going to a city so fair.
>
> I'm looking for a city
> Whose builder and maker is God.
> I'm looking for a city
> Where angel's feet do trod.
> I'm looking for a city, looking for a city
> When I die or when I fly.
> I'm going to that city;
> Going to that city in the sky.

CHAPTER 22

BEHOLD I COME QUICKLY

Verses 1-7:

1. *And he shewed me a pure river of the water of life, clear as crystal, proceeding out of the throne of God and of the Lamb.*

2. *In the midst of the street of it, and on either side of the river, was there the tree of life, which bare twelve manner of fruits, and yielded her fruit every month; and the leaves of the tree were for the healing of the nations.*

3. *And there shall be no more curse; but the throne of God and of the Lamb shall be in it; and his servants shall serve him.*

4. *And they shall see his face; and his name shall be in their foreheads.*

5. *And there shall be no night there; and they need no candle, neither light of the sun; for the Lord God giveth them light; and they shall reign forever and ever.*

6. *And he said unto me, These sayings are faithful and true; and the Lord God of the holy prophets sent his angel to shew unto his servants the things which must shortly be done.*

7. *Behold I come quickly! Blessed is he that keepeth the sayings of the prophecy of this book (Revelation).*

Three additional things are shown to John here in this chapter about the New City and its glory.

- *The River of Life: "pure...clear as crystal proceeding out of the throne of God."*

- *The Street of the City:* Note, the word *"street"* is in the singular indicating that it was the main street of the New City. Perhaps the singular represents the singular *"Lamb of God"* who Himself said, *"I am the way (street), the truth and the life!"* (John 14:6).

- *The Tree of Life:* We studied earlier that the 'Tree of Life' was originally in the beautiful creation of God in the Garden of Eden. Had humanity, male and female, chosen to eat of this tree rather than the 'Tree of Knowledge' perhaps things would have been a lot different. Only God knows, but I still say as I have throughout these writings: *God has everything under control!*

An amazing thing about this *'Tree of Life'* is that it grew up on either side of the 'River of Life'. God must have planted its roots underneath the river to forever be watered by the pure waters of the river. Another amazing thing about it is that it bore on one tree twelve different fruits. Each month a different fruit appeared in full growth upon this amazing tree. I think that it represents spiritually the *'Fruit of the Spirit'* spoken of in Galatians 5:22,23 plus some other characteristics of God's own eternal nature.

In Verse 5, we read this phrase, *"and they shall reign forever and ever."* Who are *"they"* spoken of here? The Bride sits in the throne with God the Father and Jesus Christ the Lamb.

"To him that overcometh will I grant to sit with me (Jesus the Lamb) in my throne, even as I also overcame, and am set down with my Father in his throne!" (Rev.3:21).

In verse 7, a blessing is pronounced upon all those *"that keep the sayings of the prophecy of this book."* This speaks of the book of Revelation, which we have just studied.

Three times in Chapter 22, Jesus speaks personally (red letter edition) to say, *"I COME QUICKLY!"* Let's be ready for that great day!

Verses 8-13:

8. *And I John saw these things, and heard them. And when I had heard and seen, I fell down to worship before the feet of the angel which shewed me these things.*

9. *Then saith he unto me, See thou do it not; for I am thy fellowservant, and of thy brethren the prophets, and of them which keep the sayings of this book. Worship God!*

10. *And he saith unto me, Seal not the sayings of the prophecy of this book; for the time is at hand.*

11. *He that is unjust, let him be unjust still; and he which is filthy, let him be filthy still; and he that is righteous, let him be righteous still; and he that is holy, let him be holy still.*

12. *And, behold, I come quickly; and my reward is with me to give to every man according as his work shall be.*

13. *I am Alpha and Omega, the beginning and the end, the first and the last.*

There are several very important things that we learn from this portion of Scripture.

- Don't worship angels. Only the Lord is worthy of our worship.
- Keep the Word of God. Follow what the Word says in the Book of Revelation. Be an overcomer!
- Seal *not* the prophecy of Revelation. (Verse 10).

Doesn't it seem strange that God told Daniel just the opposite. *"But thou, O Daniel, shut up the words, and seal the book, even to the time of the end."* (Dan. 12:4).

The key here is that Daniel would only be 'sealed' until the time of the end. God, in this end-time, is now revealing all of the precious truth of His Holy Word.

Verse 11 clearly shows us that we can sin away God's wonderful grace.

In verse 12, The Lord's reward is with Him at His coming.

Then in verse 13, Christ's eternal nature is once again proclaimed. *"The Alpha and Omega, the beginning and the end, the first and the last!"*. And as I have said before – *Everything in between!*

Now we come to the final verses of our study. My prayer is that you will have learned something that you did not know before. More than that I pray that you will be stirred to know that these are truly 'the last days' and we must be ready to meet Him face to face not too far from now.

Verses 14:

Blessed are they that do his commandments, that they may have a right to the tree of life, and may enter in through the gates into the city.

Adam, male and female, forfeited that right way back in the Garden of Eden when they made the wrong choice of which tree to touch and eat. You may think, as so many have been taught, that it was *"the woman whom thou gavest to be with me"* (Gen. 3:12), who was totally to blame. But look with me at what the Good Book says.

"And when the woman saw that the tree was good for food, and that it was pleasant to the eyes, and a tree to be desired to make one wise, she took of the fruit thereof, and did eat, and gave also to her husband WITH HER, and he did eat." (Gen.3:6).

I had always been taught that Adam was out somewhere tending the garden when the serpent beguiled his wife whom he later named Eve after their fall. This was not true. He was *"with her"* the whole time. Wow! What a revelation to know that women are not totally to blame after all for what we call *'the fall'*.

The promise to the righteous is that they will *"have right to the tree of life"* and to be a part of that Holy City according to this verse.

Verse 15:

For without are dogs, and sorcerers, and whoremongers, and murderers, and idolaters, and whosoever loveth and maketh a lie.

Have you ever wondered where the unrighteous and wicked are going to be in eternity. You might say, "In the lake of fire according to the Scriptures." Yes, but just where is this *"lake of fire"*? Could it be possible that it is like the city dump, just outside the New City, where those who are condemned to be there can look over and see the glory of the city that they missed. Just a thought, but maybe so.

Verses 16-21:

16. *I Jesus have sent mine angel to testify unto you these things in the churches. I am the root and offspring of David, and the bright and morning star.*

17. *And the Spirit and the bride say, Come. And let him that heareth say, Come. And let him that is athirst come. And whosoever will, let him take the water of life freely.*

18. *For I testify unto every man that heareth the words of the prophecy of this book (Revelation), if any man shall add unto these things, God shall add unto him the plagues that are written in this book.*

19. *And if any man shall take away from the words of the book of this prophecy, God shall take away his part out of the book of life, and out of the holy city, and from the things which are written in this book.*

20. *He which testifieth these things saith, Surely I come quickly. Amen. Even so, come, Lord Jesus.*

21. *The grace of our Lord Jesus Christ be with you all. Amen!*

The Old Testament ends with a curse. It says in Malachi 4:6, *"lest I come and smite the earth with a curse!"*

The New Testament, however, ends with grace and blessing for it says here, *"The grace of our Lord Jesus Christ be with you all!"* (verse 21).

Isn't it wonderful that the very last page of the Bible ends with an invitation to all who will hear God's voice and to all who are thirsty for more of Him, just to come *"and take the water of life freely."*

"Come unto me, all ye that labour and are heavy laden, and I will give you rest!" (Matt.11:30).

These precious words of our Lord Jesus are still extended today to all who will heed them. If you need Him for anything, just 'COME'.

So ends my book '*Unveiling the Apocalypse*'. I trust that it has been a blessing to you and that you have learned from it. Thank you for taking your time to have studied it with me. May God bless you everyone!

AMEN

BIBLIOGRAPHY

The Schofield Study Bible King James Version. Copyright 1909 by Oxford University Press, Inc. New York, New York.

Strong's Exhaustive Concordance, Dr. James Strong. Reprint Edition 1997 by Baker Book House Co. Grand Rapids, Michigan.

Revelation by Dr. M. R. De Haan. Copyright 1946 by Zondervan Publishing House. Grand Rapids, Michigan.

An Exposition of the Seven Church Ages. Written by William Marrion Branham. Published 1965 by the Branham Tabernacle. Jeffersonville, Indiana.

Lectures on the Book of Revelation by H. A. Ironside. Copyright 1930 by Loizeaux Brothers. Neptune, New Jersey.

Studies in Revelation by J. Narver Gortner. Copyright 1948 by the Gospel Publishing House. Springfield, Missouri.

Jesus Is Coming by W.E.B. Copyright 1898,1908, 1932 by Fleming H. Revell Co. New York, New York.

Revelation Books 1-4 by B.R. Hicks. Copyright 1973-1991 by Christ Gospel Press. Jeffersonville, Indiana.

The Sign by Robert Van Kampen. Copyright 1992 by Crossway Books, Wheaton, Illinois.

www.ingramcontent.com/pod-product-compliance
Lightning Source LLC
Chambersburg PA
CBHW051952150726
47999CB00004B/1352